Second Edition

MILLENNIAL ENGAGEMENT
IN THE WORKPLACE

Finding Common Ground to
Bridge the Multi-Generational Gap

MARK E. CANER

Table of Contents

INTRODUCTION

"The children now love luxury; they often show disrespect for elders and love chatter in place of exercise. They no longer rise when their elders enter the room. They contradict their parents, chatter before company, cross their legs, and tyrannize their teachers."

As you examine this quote, which generation immediately comes to mind? Do not be too quick to judge because you may be surprised. Although this depiction may contain characteristics of the Millennial generation, the quote goes all the way back to the Fourth Century philosopher Socrates. Hence, although we may feel this generation pushes the envelope on decorum, it may not be as distinct as we think. Moreover, it is important to remember that they are a product of their upbringing. So the parents of this generation, who primarily consist of Baby Boomers, are significant contributors to such behavior.

When we consider this dynamic with research that strongly indicates that most of our cultural lens (i.e. learned perspective during our upbringing) is nearly developed and set by age 17, it makes it imperative to understand a Millennial's formative youth before we can examine their proclivities in the workforce. Thus, although the intent of this book is to enable organizational leaders and Millennials to find common ground to bridge the multi-generational workforce gaps that exist, it will need to first seek to understand who they are and what their modus operandi is before a strategy or best practice is proposed.

Accordingly, this book has taken this challenge to task by surveying Millennials from private sector corporations, educational institutions and charitable organizations in order to evaluate, measure and analyze its results with a wealth of generational research that has been conducted since they formally entered the workforce over the last decade.

During the first edition of this book (written in 2013), this survey was distributed to Millennials between age 22 and 30 from several Fortune 500 corporations, Division I-A universities, and charitable organizations. At that time, younger Millennials (less than age 22) were excluded to disregard jobs held during undergraduate studies or prior to the beginning of their first vocations. Thus, although this definition does not assure that these results are decisively accurate, this was the most common designated age utilized in the Millennial research encountered. In total, there were 230 responses that were received from Millennials in private sector businesses (e.g. Western & Southern Financial Group, Nationwide Insurance, Fifth Third Bank), alumni associations from universities (e.g., Ohio State, Duke, Indiana, Notre Dame), and young, emerging leaders from charitable organizations (e.g., Salvation Army Echelon, Young Leaders from American Red Cross).

The survey consisted of 16 questions ranging from multiple choice to open-ended inquiries. It focused on discerning their preference for communication (e.g. synchronous versus e-mail or online), frequency of interaction with their manager (with an emphasis on performance reviews) and ranking of career priorities (e.g., work environment, work life balance, career progression, challenging assignment, and pay/benefits). Once their preferences were selected, the survey empowered them to elaborate on their responses, such as portraying what the ultimate work-life balance would look like, describing the ideal work environment and explaining what constitutes "fair" pay/benefits from their perspective. Moreover, it provided a glimpse into how loyal they are to their employers and what key factors contribute to their longevity to remain with the same organization.

It is important to note the survey's absolute commitment to keep their responses anonymous. This assurance, which was pledged by alumni members and trusted officials, facilitated candid insights into how an organization can meet the needs of the Millennial.

Moreover, the survey made discernable advancements with enlightening insights, organizational strategies and best practices that leaders could employ to improve issues that have been identified by the Millennials within their workplace. Ultimately, it proved to be an acutely valuable tool to more effectively comprehend the Millennial's mindset in order to align it with an organization's mission, vision and values. Although there is not nor will there ever be perfect alignment, this survey combined with the extensive research that has come to light over the last decade, can serve as the impetus toward bridging gaps that exist between today's organizations and the Millennials by finding common ground.

Chapter One

A Portrait of the Millennials

"Millennials really do seem to want everything, and I can't decide if it's an inability or an unwillingness to make trade-offs," says Derrick Bolton, assistant dean and M.B.A. admissions director at Stanford University's Graduate School of Business. "They want to be CEO, for example, but they say they don't want to give up time with their families."

This quote from *The Wall Street Journal* summarizes a common perception many have about the Millennial generation. They seem to want everything and have a sense of entitlement. Moreover, they demand more from companies than prior generations, yet are less loyal. This issue, along with many other topics relating to the Millennial generation, will be explored throughout this chapter in order to garner an incisive and accurate sense of who they are and what contributing factors were behind their resulting development.

First and foremost, it is central to define the age band of this generation. Although the inaugural age of this generation is unequivocally clear (i.e., those born after 1981), researchers in some studies disagree on the end date. This is the first generation to come of age in the new millennium so the commencement date is set. In 2018 Pew Research, the source of much of the research this book cites, concluded that it should subsequently use 1996 as its end date for the Millennial generation. This range is equivalent in age span to their preceding generation. Moreover, Pew determined that a 1996 end date would allow the entire Millennial generation to have had formative memories of key political, economic and social factors such as the 9/11 terrorist attacks that shook our nation and the 2008 U.S. presidential election. Both of these events had historical significance for the Millennials.

The entire generational spectrum that Pew envisions is as follows:

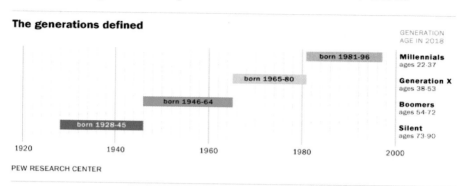

The generations defined

PEW RESEARCH CENTER

Within this age band, there are approximately 75 million people in the United States that are considered Millennials. With Pew's 1996 end date, all Millennials are old enough now to have either entered the work force, or to be pursuing education or training to improve their outcomes once they enter it. Removing Millennials who are pursuing education or training, or who are not working or actively seeking work for other reasons, and using Bureau of Labor statistics, Pew estimated there are 56 million Millennials in the work force today. This number is large enough to give Millennials the distinction of having obtained greater work force numbers than the generations which preceded them:

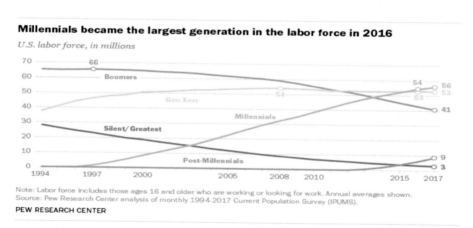

Millennials became the largest generation in the labor force in 2016

U.S. labor force, in millions

Note: Labor force includes those ages 16 and older who are working or looking for work. Annual averages shown.
Source: Pew Research Center analysis of monthly 1994-2017 Current Population Survey (IPUMS).
PEW RESEARCH CENTER

With its oldest members now exceeding 15 years in the workforce, Millennials have started to mark their passage with a distinct personality. They appear confident, self-expressive, liberal, upbeat and open to change. By and large, they are more ethnically and racially diverse than older adults, which Brookings shows in Figure 1 using 2015 Census Bureau Estimates.

Figure 1: US Race-Ethnic Profiles for Age Groups, 2015

Source: William H Frey analysis of Census Bureau Estimates released June 23, 2016

B | Metropolitan Policy Program
at BROOKINGS

As illustrated in this diagram, racial and ethnic minorities currently make up 44 percent of the Millennials, which compares to 38 percent of Gen Xers, and only 25 percent of the older generations. Another unique Millennial demographic is their nativity. Roughly 11 percent of all Millennials are U.S.-born children of at least one immigrant parent, which is much higher than Gen Xers (7 percent) and Boomers (5 percent). This resembles the Silent generation (11 percent), whose parents also came to the United States during a surge of immigration.

Another important difference of Millennials, particularly in the workforce, is their level of education. The following Pew Research charts present how Millennials compare to previous generations, with other demographics being reflected as well:

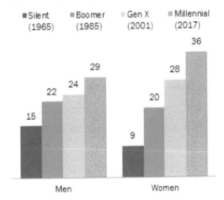

As young adults, Millennials more educated than previous generations

% of those ages 21 to 36 who have completed at least a bachelor's degree, by gender

■ Silent (1965)   ■ Boomer (1985)   Gen X (2001)   ■ Millennial (2017)

Note: The educational attainment question was changed in 1992. For Boomers and Silents, the share shown refers those who completed at least four years of college (regardless of degree status).
Source: Pew Research Center tabulations of the 1965, 1985, 2001 and 2017 Current Population Survey Annual Social and Economic Supplement (ASEC) from the Integrated Public Use Microdata Series (IPUMS)

PEW RESEARCH CENTER

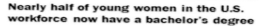

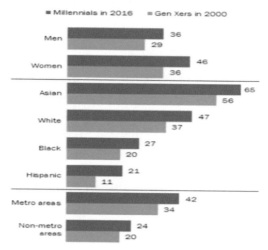

Nearly half of young women in the U.S. workforce now have a bachelor's degree

% of employed 25- to 29-year-olds with a bachelor's degree or more

■ Millennials in 2016   ■ Gen Xers in 2000

Category	Millennials in 2016	Gen Xers in 2000
Men	36	29
Women	46	36
Asian	65	56
White	47	37
Black	27	20
Hispanic	21	11
Metro areas	42	34
Non-metro areas	24	20

Note: "Employed" refers to those who were at work in the week prior to survey or were temporarily absent from their jobs. Whites, blacks and Asians include only non-Hispanics. Hispanics are of any race.
Source: Pew Research Center analysis of 2000 and 2016 Current Population Survey Annual Social and Economic Supplements (IPUMS).

PEW RESEARCH CENTER

Based on education attainment at the same age, the percentage of Millennials who have completed college considerably outpaces older generations, even their next oldest "sibling," the Gen Xers. For 18-24 year-olds in the early 1990s, NCES statistics showed about 34 percent were enrolled in college. This had climbed to 41 percent by 2009, when Millennials averaged about the same age. Moreover, a survey earlier this decade showed that more than half of the Millennials have at least some college education (54 percent), compared to 49 percent of Gen Xers, 36 percent of Boomers and 24 percent of the Silent generation when they were ages 18 to 28. Statistically, Millennials are also more likely to have completed high school than the previous generations.

Millennial women have surpassed Millennial men in the share graduating from or attending college, a trend that began during the Gen X generation. Conversely, in the Boomer and Silent generations, men had exceeded women in college attendance and graduation. Unfortunately, the above chart also shows Black and Hispanic Millennials significantly trailing their Asian and White counterparts in this educational attainment. Correcting this is arguably an important societal goal, as Brookings estimates that racial and ethnic minorities will comprise 50 percent of the U.S. population by the mid-2040s.

Hence, the Millennials are the most educated generation in American history. However, this has not led to being gainfully employed, though things have improved considerably since the 2008-2009 "Great Recession," as the chart below illustrates. Nevertheless, a consistent theme is higher unemployment than earlier generations had experienced at the same age.

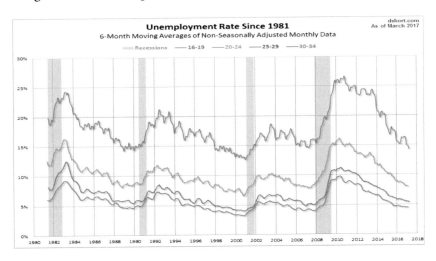

Another trend, which is tied to the decades-long trend to increased education, is the declining percentage of 18 to 32 year-olds who are married, as seen in the following Pew Research study released in 2014:

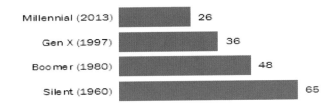

5

Compared with the Silent generation at the same age (18 to 32), Millennials are more likely to be in the labor force due a preference by the younger women in the Silent generation to be stay-at-home wives. Millennials do not necessarily have less desire to be married, as Pew notes 69 percent of currently unmarried Millennials have an intention to eventually marry, but presently believe they lack the necessary economic foundation.

Another factor that needs to be understood when analyzing this demographic shift with Millennials is the makeup of the household. Although some may leap to assume that a single-person household has replaced the married-with-children family unit of the past, research has shown this contention to be utterly false. In 2014, Pew found that more 18 to 34 year-olds live at home than those are married or co-habiting in a separate household. Many Millennials choose to live with other family members, such as their parents, particularly when returning from college. This act has earned them the nickname of the "Boomerang" generation. Additionally, many Millennials choose to remain in their parents' home until they get married to save on expenses given the challenging economy and ability to remain gainfully employed. Moreover, when they do decide to move out of their parents' home, they usually elect to live with a roommate, rather than on their own.

In addition to the Great Recession, many pejorative events have transpired during Millennials lives that have shaped them, such the terror attacks of September 11, 2001, the subsequent wars that have resulted from this event and the Lost Decade in the stock market which netted zero growth during their generation's entire investment horizon. In spite of this, there is strong evidence that Millennials are optimistic as a generation, in spite of often meager prospects for the present. This can be seen in the 2014 Pew Research chart.

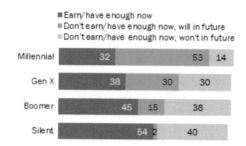

Millennials Upbeat about Their Financial Future

% saying they ... to lead the kind of life they want

- Earn/have enough now
- Don't earn/have enough now, will in future
- Don't earn/have enough now, won't in future

	Earn/have enough now	Don't earn/have enough now, will in future	Don't earn/have enough now, won't in future
Millennial	32	53	14
Gen X	38	30	30
Boomer	45	15	38
Silent	54	2	40

Note: Based on all adults regardless of employment status. N=1,821. Those who are employed were asked if they currently or will "earn enough money" and those who are not employed were asked if they currently or will "have enough income." "Don't know/Refused" responses not shown.

Source: Pew Research survey, Feb. 14-23, 2014

PEW RESEARCH CENTER

Similarly, with the question of whether "the country's best years are ahead", Pew Research found that 49 percent of the Millennial generation answered affirmatively, compared to 42 percent of Gen X, 44 percent of Baby Boomers and 39 percent of the Silent generation.

As with all generations, there are moments in time as well as unique qualities that will ultimately define who they are. When they were asked what makes them distinctive, Millennials overwhelmingly answered *technology use.* Should this response stun us when considering they are history's first "always connected" generation? Although all modern generations eventually embraced technology to some extent, Millennials have noticeably outpaced other generations in terms of their frequency of use, even as older generations are beginning to "catch up," as shown in the chart below. When studying technology as a whole, the big difference between Millennials and other generations is connectivity. Although all generations will connect themselves to technology to some extent, the Millennial generation will continuously keep themselves connected to their technology.

	Millennials (23-41)	Gen-X (42-53)	Boomers (54-72)	Silent (73+)
Internet Behaviors				
Use Social Media	85%	75%	57%	23%
Use Facebook	82%	76%	59%	26%
Computer and Cell Phone Ownership				
Own a smart phone	92%	85%	67%	30%
Own a desktop	57%	69%	65%	–
Own a laptop	54%	64%	52%	25%
Own a tablet	5%	5%	4%	–

Sources: Karr, Douglas. (2017). *How Each Generation Has Adapted To and Utilizes Technology.* Indianapolis, IN: MarTech/DK New Media. Jiang, Jingjing. (2018). *Millennials Stand Out for Their Technology Use, But Older Generations Also Embrace Digital Life.* Washington D.C.: Pew Research Center. Global Web Index. (2018). *Examining the Attitudes and Digital Behaviors of Internet Users Aged 21-34.* New York, NY: Global Web Index.

Some other psychographic characteristics of Millennials in the workforce are their expectations to have a voice, desire for instant gratification, self-expression through body art and piercings, hunger for recognition and goal-oriented mindset. A good example of a culture that would greatly frustrate a Millennial is an assembly line when all decisions are preemptively made for them. They desire to provide input and customize solutions, rather than follow a prescribed strategy. They would prefer to engage with management in some of the solutions and share ideas to problems. Moreover, given their upbringing during an era when information is available 24/7 via the Internet, the news networks and interactive technology, they have grown accustomed to accessing information instantly and easily.

Their recurrent desire for self expression demonstrates their individuality through body art and piercings. For instance, a recent study found nearly 40 percent of Millennials had at least one tattoo, of which half had multiple tattoos. Likewise, almost 25 percent of those surveyed had a piercing in some place other than their earlobe, which is practically six times greater than older adults. Although tattoos are very common, they are almost always beneath clothing.

As a generation, Millennials have expressed a growing need for frequent feedback from their manager, particularly when it involves recognition of their accolades. The type and frequency of feedback required will be covered in depth in Chapter Eight. However, it suffices to say that their craving for instant gratification and strong hunger for recognition is intensely greater than that of prior generations. To that end, research has revealed that a popular technique to meet these insatiable needs is positive reinforcement (for successes and coaching opportunities) and constant recognition of laudable achievements. Clearly, these identified issues will have vast implications for managing this generation relative to the current practice (i.e., annual merit, semi-annual review) in place for older generations.

As noted in the initial commentary of this chapter, there continues to be a growing concern that Millennials demand more from organizations than the other generations, yet are less loyal. Given the frequency organizations have experience with Millennials "job hopping" in their first decade in the workforce, it is easy to understand why some of them are growing increasingly frustrated with this new generation. The facts are daunting when considering Millennials have averaged 6.2 job changes by age 26, according to the Bureau of Labor Statistics. This tendency is exacerbated by separate research showing that 26 percent of Millennials have been laid off at one time or another, and 47 percent of Millennials anticipate needing a second source of income or a second job at some point.

A 2017 Qualtrics study indicated that 74 percent of Millennials who like their jobs were planning to leave within the next three years. To give insight into the likely primary reasons, Qualtrics surveyed Millennials who had recently left their jobs while also having liked them. Qualtrics found that 36 percent left for a better opportunity, 24 percent left because of a need/desire to re-locate, 16 percent left because of going back to school, 14 percent left to learn new skills and 10 percent left to change fields. In a 2017 article commenting on this survey, *Forbes* notes that companies might want to address the first, second and fourth cited reasons by respectively providing more "upward mobility" opportunities, more opportunities to work remotely and more internal training. Furthermore, this same Qualtrics survey indicated 89 percent of Millennials would expect to stay in their present job for 10 years, if there were opportunities for upward career mobility which included increases in their compensation. This issue is explored in greater detail in Chapter Nine to determine what it will take to instill loyalty in Millennials.

There is a significant amount of generational research that clearly indicates we are in fact products of our upbringing. For example, two prominent thought leaders on global societies, Drs. Javidan and House, argue that our adult values and cultural lens is virtually developed and established by age 17. Thus, it is imperative to understand the tremendous influence the parents of Millennials have had in shaping their development. To start, the parents of this generation (which were primarily Baby Boomers) were intensely involved in their lives. As a matter of fact, many of the parents actually sought to be their kid's friends. This prescriptive style, which was more apparent than in any prior generation, is what earned Millennials another nickname, "The Scripted Generation." The script that was written for them by their parents sounded something like this, "You can be anything you want to be" and "You are unique and special."

In other words, the Boomers created an environment where everyone was treated remarkably special and everyone was a winner, which is what ultimately labeled them as "The Trophy Generation." The result of this cultural environment was a generation that became confident, ambitious and individualistic with high expectations. However, to a person that hasn't taken the time to fully understand who they are and their upbringing, Millennials can be *perceived* as over-confident, impatient, and entitled people who lack loyalty to anyone but themselves. Hence, Baby Boomers focused a great deal of attention on raising their Millennial children as individuals, and not as part of a group. Thus, it was this concentration on uniqueness and individuality that led to their eventual development.

Ultimately, it was this upbringing that netted the generation we now know as the Millennials. This background is not only useful to understand the Millennial perspective, but has important organizational implications, which will be discussed in future chapters.

Now that we have taken the time to truly understand who the Millennials are, this book will now focus on how to more effectively bridge "gaps" that manifest between an employee from this generation and their employer. In order to gain a candid and practical understanding to this effort, the research cited was thoroughly vetted in an effort to avoid hasty generalizations, maintain objectivity free of assertions and substantiate all evidence.

Chapter Two

Setting the Record Straight

"Parents have coddled and overprotected their children more over the generations and have taught them, intentionally or not, to expect special treatment just for being them. This, in combination with the self-esteem movement in the schools, has likely resulted in increased narcissistic tendencies in our youth."

This quote from an article by the Discovery News Channel ultimately goes on to make the egregious claim that Millennials are the most narcissistic generation on record. This bold assertion, which is made relative to prior generations, is a common belief held by many. Is this a statement that can be substantiated or is it merely a contention without merit? This question, along with a few others, will be explored throughout this chapter to set the record straight on Millennials' narcissistic predisposition and sense of entitlement.

This Millennial charge toward narcissistic tendencies has significant implications in the workplace if it turns out to be authentic. Not only does this character flaw call into question a Millennial's judgment as it relates to their leadership, but it limits their ability to work selflessly in a team. To that end, this defect would make it incredibly challenging for businesses to find Millennials with the highly desirable "Level 5" leadership attribute, which Jim Collins defines as an employee's special capability to put their organization's interests before their own in his book "Good to Great." Thus, if this claim is true, there is clearly a reason for trepidation by organizations as they begin to hire their future leaders.

Although the intent of this analysis is to discern whether this assertion is factual, by and large it suffices to say that it would behoove any organization to explore whether a narcissistic predisposition exists in candidates (of any generation) they are interviewing for employment, particularly for leadership positions, given these striking consequences.

One study that demonstrated some evidence for this contention was conducted by San Diego State University (SDSU) over 25 years. During this period, five psychologists surveyed students between the ages 18 and 25 regarding how they wish to live their lives relative to others. The nearly 17,000 college students who participated in the "Narcissistic Personality Inventory Study" were engaged to assess their selfish tendencies. When this initiative was launched in the 1980s, Gen Xers were the target of the questions. Although the replies from this generation had some positive responses, it was far from a majority. Conversely, Millennial students responded overwhelmingly affirmative to statements such as, "I can live my life the way I want to." As a matter of fact, over two-thirds of Millennial students had an assenting reply to similar questions, which is more than 30 percent higher than the Gen Xers that were engaged earlier in the study. Thus, results like these in 2007 prompted *The New York Sun* to label the Millennial generation as the most narcissistic ever. Although the SDSU study was last conducted in 2010, its main author Jean Twenge maintains that little has really changed, citing an example from a 2016 *Psychology Today* article about a 25-year-old Yelp employee who was fired after directly contacting the company's CEO to complain about (among other things) being required to remain in an entry level position for an entire year.

Another factor that has contributed to this perception of the Millennial generation being self-absorbed is their upbringing. Keep in mind that the predominant Baby Boomer parents that raised Millennials used a nurturing parenting style, which was a subtle shift from training. This is not to say that Boomers abandoned training their children. Rather, it means that they placed more emphasis on nurturing by espousing positive affirmation and attention with them. As a result, Millennials have developed a desire for managers in the workplace that tend to their career development while acting as an advocate for them. To that end, it is important that organizations consider this when managing Millennials in order to more effectively coach them. As a result, a few of the chapters in this book will dedicate more attention to this topic by providing some practical tips and applications.

In order to truly understand the "nurturing" parental style that transpired during the Millennial's upbringing, it is important to examine the source of this paradigm shift. One of the greatest contributors was Dr. Benjamin Spock. In his handbook on childcare, Dr. Spock convinced a new generation of parents that coddling babies when they cried and showering affection upon them would only make them happier and more secure. This approach was counter to the prevailing point of view that it is best not to pick up a crying baby because doing so would ultimately spoil them. Moreover, Spock urged parents to be flexible and see their children as individuals, rather than use a one-size-fits-all approach.

As unique as these techniques seemed, the most revolutionary suggestion he had for parents was to be "friends" with their kids. This merriment approach was completely at odds with the cold authoritarianism that had been favored by most parenting books of the time. Hence, Spock's parental lessons were widely used by Boomers and played an integral role influencing the development of the Millennials. Thus, this factor has to be considered to fully understand the "nurturing" parental style that became omnipresent.

In order to collect both perspectives of the claim that Millennials are narcissistic, studies focusing on their altruistic propensity by The Pew Research Center and Rutgers University were examined. The Pew survey concluded that Millennials placed a higher value in focusing on others (more often than themselves) as it related to their marriage, children and community. The Rutgers University research observed Millennials actions, as opposed to their intentions as Pew's survey had done. Their investigation found that approximately 80% of Millennial high school students voluntarily participated in some form of community service, which is significantly higher than the previous generations they had studied. Thus, these studies witnessed selfless tendencies in intent and action. More recently, the 2015 Millennial impact study found 84 percent of Millennials had made a charitable cash donation in 2014, with 78 percent doing so apart from payroll deduction. It also found 70 percent of Millennials volunteered time in 2014 with 10 percent of them volunteering more than 40 hours, which demonstrates some altruism.

Hence, when both sides of this narcissistic claim are taken into consideration and balanced with the cultural influence of this day and age, it is difficult at best to make this egregious contention. Moreover, when narcissism is defined as "an inordinate fascination with oneself, excessive self-love or vanity," it can be problematic to make this indictment on an entire generation considering the exculpatory evidence that was offered by the Pew Research Center and Rutgers University. Conversely, based on the SDSU study over a 25-year period, it would not be a stretch to reason they are perhaps over confident with very high self-esteem. Thus, although it would be a hasty generalization to contend that Millennials are narcissistic, by and large, there are certainly traces of this disposition that can be found within individuals of this generation. When found in employees within your workplace, it is important to eliminate these tendencies for the sake of teamwork.

For organizational leaders, a best practice that can help your Millennial associates understand why a self-absorbed predisposition is unhealthy for the business is to take the time to engage with them about the big picture. In other words, describe what ultimately needs to be achieved and get their input. Not only do Millennials want to feel "involved," but they greatly appreciate the opportunity to be mentored (more on this topic in chapter eight). For Millennial associates, it is important for them to recognize the experience their leaders have when various situations arise. Although many have taken the time to get an advanced education to prepare them for the workforce, this can not serve as a substitute for the real-time experience many leaders have garnered over the years. Hence, it is this "wisdom" that has earned them the trust of an organization's senior management to lead its business unit. For older leaders and Millennials, it is vital to remember they both need each other (working collegially together) to achieve the best results for the organization.

Another widespread contention that should be examined, particularly as it relates to the workplace, is the Millennial generation's overt sense of entitlement. This common perception was reported by *The Wall Street Journal* in 2008 based on a survey conducted by CareerBuilder.com. In the report, more than 85 percent of human resource executives and hiring managers said they felt Millennials have a stronger sense of entitlement than older workers. When dissecting this attitude as it relates to the workplace, it refers to their self-perceived mind set that they deserve to be recognized and rewarded. Likewise, they want to move up the corporate ladder expeditiously, but not always on management's terms. They want a guarantee for their performance, not just the opportunity to perform. To that end, a 2017 *Forbes* study found Millennial entitlement has the potential benefit of driving creativity and independence, in accordance to the value they ascribe themselves. However, the research also indicated the attendant downside risk of propensity to demand higher pay and a perceived permission to bend, usurp or override their employer's rules.

There were additional research studies that supported this claim, such as Michigan State University's Collegiate Employment Research Institute and MonsterTrak, an online career site. In their studies, they surveyed Millennial associates in the workplace and found that nearly half of the participants had a relatively high feeling of superiority about themselves. Their grade factor was measured by Millennials responding affirmatively to statements such as, "I know that I have more natural talents than most." In addition, their research went on to argue that a Millennial's sense of entitlement has been ingrained in them by their parents, and therefore will always exist to some extent.

Thus, given this evidence, could it be that this sense of entitlement is merely the result of the Millennial's upbringing? By raising them with an expectation to receive an award or trophy for simply participating, rather than merit, the parents of this "Trophy Generation" have apparently instilled this within them, whether it was deliberate or not. Hence, although it may be difficult to make this claim as a hard fact due to subjectivity, there is no doubt that this is the perception today, which is quickly becoming the reality.

Some authors have countered this entitlement claim against Millennials based on interpretation. For instance, Morley Winograd and Michael Hais, authors of the popular book "Millennial Momentum," are quick to point out that the Millennial generation by and large does not perceive itself in this way. In contrast, they view their comments as conversations that they have grown accustomed to having with their parents. From their cultural lens, they are merely negotiating with their employer when they seek work/life balance via flexible hours. On the contrary, many employers view this "dialogue" as a demand, rather than a request. Hence, this breakdown has produced a misunderstanding between Millennial workers and organizational leaders from this disconnect in empathy.

Although many Millennials clearly consider the evidence to the entitlement claim inconclusive, this perception by the older workers has become a reality in the workplace. This phenomenon has not been limited to Corporate America, but has also played out in other parts of society, such as sports. In order to fully understand the prevalence of these incidents, it may be helpful to observe this dynamic from outside your industry. A good example of this breakdown between Millennials and older workers occurred on a segment of HBO's "Inside the NFL" a few years ago. In this particular case, the story was about a current NFL player (from the Millennial generation) that had taken off nine days during the season when his grandmother passed away. As a result of his actions, his team fined him due to what it considered an excessive amount of time off. The fine was ultimately overturned when the league was petitioned by the NFL Players Association, which successfully argued the time take was within the player's rights.

The most interesting dynamic was the reaction of broadcast commentators to the situation. All of them were of a different generation with experiences to match. None of them could believe the player showed this type of disrespect for the league with his sense of "entitlement." Moreover, the commentators, who had all been successful NFL football players in their day, considered this an act that ultimately let down his teammates. On the other hand, the player himself considered his nine days off to just be "work-life" balance. He considered it to be a reverent display of affection for his family, as well as a discipline to prevent his work from interfering with his priority with family. So how can it be that these two generations can have such different viewpoints of this same act? Perspective!

What one generation considers improper may be viewed by another as decorum. This example should be an alarm to what happens when we compare ourselves to others without understanding their perspective, particularly when generational differences exist. Thus, the next time leaders find themselves in a similar situation, remember this lesson. It can have like applications in the workplace, especially when multi-generational workers are involved. Hence, a best practice for Millennial associates with regard to this sense of entitlement is Stephen Covey's Fifth Habit: "Seek First to Understand *before* Seeking to be Understood." In other words, Millennials may want to try to empathetically appreciate an older associate's point of view before they pass judgment. Based on this research, it is apparent that some Millennials' comments may be misinterpreted as narcissistic by some of the elder associates they work with. This is something Millennials should bear in mind.

In addition, it would behoove Millennial associates to temper their expectations in the workplace, especially when they are in a role where they do not have vast experience. By the same token, organizational leaders should also adopt the same Covey principle of "seeking to understand before being understood" and affirm where appropriate Millennial attributes like the following factors, which were identified in a 2017 Wells Fargo study:

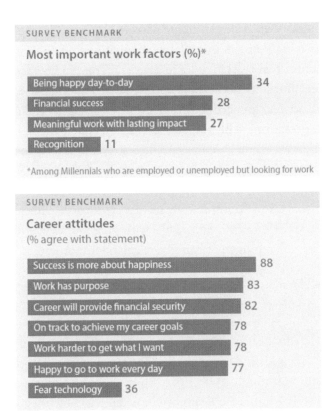

SURVEY BENCHMARK

Most important work factors (%)*

Being happy day-to-day	34
Financial success	28
Meaningful work with lasting impact	27
Recognition	11

*Among Millennials who are employed or unemployed but looking for work

SURVEY BENCHMARK

Career attitudes
(% agree with statement)

Success is more about happiness	88
Work has purpose	83
Career will provide financial security	82
On track to achieve my career goals	78
Work harder to get what I want	78
Happy to go to work every day	77
Fear technology	36

Hence, it is always in an organizational leader's best interest to learn more about their associates, especially the younger ones that they have not worked with a great deal, before they pass judgment. In America, we believe our philosophical entitlements are for life, liberty and the pursuit of happiness. Conversely, everything else...must be earned.

The final section of this chapter will address miscellaneous common myths about the Millennial generation's attitude toward work and career. In practically all these cases, what some people may perceive as a myth is simply a misunderstanding about the reality.

Myth #1: Millennials are disloyal and unwilling to make a real commitment to employers

Reality: Millennials do not exhibit categorical loyalty, but they do tender transactional loyalty, which is defined as a conditional allegiance based on what they can negotiate. Thus, organizational leaders will likely need to clearly define what is "expected" of their Millennial associates at the onset of their relationship (almost a pseudo-contractual pact) in order to assure that the employment conditions are mutually acceptable to both parties. Likewise, Millennial associates will need to take the time to understand their manager's expectations with respect to employment conditions to assure they are on the same page. Ultimately, all negotiations should be complete before they commence their relationship. Subsequently, a 2017 CNBC study suggests Millennials will then expect their managers to communicate an expected career path regularly that good performance will enable, with such investment in the first 90 days of employment being particularly important.

Myth #2: Millennials need work to be fun and require much flexibility in the workplace

Reality: Millennials want work to be engaging. They want to learn, to be challenged, and to understand the overall mission of the organization. Although some insist on a lax work environment, most merely want some flexibility in when and how they work. Thus, organizational leaders should clearly understand these preferences and demands in advance of hiring Millennials to assure they are aligned with the organization's culture. Likewise, Millennial associates need to think through their non-negotiable matters before they agree to employment. If they are not content with the terms early on, they will likely not be once they settle in. Furthermore, it is imperative for Millennial associates to make a commitment to the corporate culture and not assume they can change it prospectively.

Myth #3: Money and traditional benefits don't matter to Millennial generation associates

Reality: Millennials are generally quite savvy at comparing employment offers, which includes pay and benefits. However, for this generation, money and benefits are only a threshold issue. In other words, if an employer does not offer a competitive salary and benefits package, they will likely withdraw their interest without "fair" table stakes. Thus, Millennial associates must be comfortable with their pay and benefit package at the onset. Once onboard, they will not expect to renegotiate their terms outside of the organization's traditional merit increases. For organizational leaders, take the time to understand Millennial associates' expectations in order to remain in the running for the candidate during the interview process. As referenced, this issue is table stakes to them.

Myth #4: Millennials do not have respect for their elders, particularly at their workplace

Reality: As a result of their upbringing, they are closer to their parents than any other generation has ever been. Recall that many grew up with their parents treating them as a friend. This casual relationship has translated to more casual interactions with their elders, which is viewed by some as disrespectful, where to them it is merely informal. Thus, Millennial associates need to understand that their casual interactions with elderly colleagues in the workplace is viewed as disrespectful by some. Regardless whether it is intentional, this is something they need to be cognitive of and seek a more effective way to communicate with them when it is an issue. For organizational leaders, it is central to their coexistence in the workplace that they work with Millennials that are guilty of this generational confusion. One method that has proven to work well for some is to mentor them regarding the implications of their interactions. Ultimately, it is important that they view this direction as a "mutually beneficial" learning experience for their career.

The purpose for this chapter is to set the record straight with regard to some of the myths and truths about the Millennial generation, particularly in the workplace. Although it is clearly not all inclusive, the research and findings revealed can serve as a foundation for beginning to more effectively understand some of the generational misunderstandings and differences that exist in the workplace. For organizational leaders, these new insights can provide a basis to build upon when working with and mentoring the future leaders of your company. Moreover, this clarification about Millennials is intended to empower you to tackle the issues that make managing them so challenging. Likewise, for the Millennial associates, the exposition revealed throughout this chapter is intended to prepare them for greater success by enlightening them to blind spots in their disposition (and implications) for which they may not be aware. Additionally, these insights will educate organizational leaders about Millennial perspectives to assure it is taken into consideration when being coached and managed at the workplace.

Chapter Three

Speaking the Millennial Language

"The single biggest problem in communication is the illusion that it has taken place."

This quote from Mohandas Gandhi illustrates how problematic it can be to convey a message effectively with someone. When we amalgamate multiple generations into this equation, we exponentially increase the difficulty and complexity of the language barrier. Anytime there is a younger generation entering the workplace in large numbers, as is the case today with Millennials, there are destined to be language conflicts. To that end, it is not unusual for a new generation to seek ways (through slang) to differentiate themselves from older generations. Hence, inevitable distinctions will evolve in jargon and language.

In addition to their burning desire for independence by distinguishing themselves from their parents, Millennial generational differences can similarly be explained by the environment in which they were raised. Nonetheless, nowhere is this divergence between generations more apparent than in *how* they use language. Regardless of how unique this might appear, this distinction has existed in every generation since the beginning of time.

As a result of their experiences, upbringing, and events that have occurred during their lifetime, Millennials communicate with each other using a rich mixture of technical jargon, slang language, colloquialisms, and chat speak. However, it is important to bear in mind that it is the way words are used, paired together and perceived that *changes* with generations and not necessarily the language itself. For instance, calling a guy "cat" has a unique meaning for Boomers. Likewise, Gen Xers use the word "psyched" in a different context than other generations. Once in a while, old slangs will get resurrected to become "cool" again. An example of a phrase that has revived from Boomers to

Millennials are "groovy" and "right on." These terms have skipped a generation to become "hip" again.

An example of a national event that created generational language for Millennials is the Columbine High School massacre, where 2 deranged teen killed 12 students and a teacher. Although this tragedy affected people of all generations, some of the expressions that have evolved from this incident are unique to Millennials, such as "before you go all Columbine, relax" to reference someone going on a violent rampage or getting bent out of shape. Consequently, Millennials can appear at times to be speaking another language to their elder colleagues. Hence, it is imperative for an organizational leader working in a multigenerational environment to understand the context of evolving dialect, particularly for the new generation entering the workplace. Similarly, Millennials need to be mindful of the generational dialect they use that can be confusing to elder colleagues. Moreover, it would behoove Millennial associates to avoid using "casual" language in the workplace.

Millennials are also responsible for freshly minted technical jargon that, to a large extent, was coined by the computer programmers of this generation, yet spilled over into their everyday life. The following are examples that were embellished by the Millennials:

- **Compunicate** – according to urbandictionary.com, this is when two people in the same room talk to each other through text messaging, rather than a face-to-face conversation.

- **Defriend** – according to urbandicationary.com, this occurs when you remove someone from your address book or list of contacts on a social networking site such as Facebook.

- **Lifestreaming** – according to urbandicationary.com, this is an online posting (or blog) of a person's daily activities in minute detail to make them seem important to followers.

- **Moofer** – according to urbandicationary.com, this is a term used to describe a person in a slightly degrading manner, but paradoxically as a friendly greeting or casual gesture.

These terms are often used by Millennials to fellow cohorts to demonstrate they are "in." Although these terms may seem pretty casual to a non-Millennial and hence, have limited application in the workplace, keep in mind that this younger generation often uses informal vernacular in their personal *and* professional life. Thus, this generational jargon can play a central role in organizations for leaders and associates alike. While Millennials are certainly not the only affinity group to use generational language, their terms are not as well known in the workplace since they have had less exposure than prior generation's slang. In addition, it is also likely that other generations may not understand their context.

Another distinctive is the Millennial Generation's use of "SMS English" which is an abbreviation for short message system. This method, which is also commonly referred to as *text talk*, is arguably the Millennial generation's most unique and defining use of language. In essence, it refers to the truncated form of communication that is used in delivery systems, such as a text message, an e-mail and instant messaging.SMS communication can come in the form of numeric code and symbols, which are frequently referred to as emoticons. Some examples of numeric codes are as follows:

"143" which translates to *I love you*, "1432" which means *I love you too*, or "411" which is cryptogram for information. Millennials will also use the numerals 2 and 4 in place of the words "to" and "for" in messages. In fact, a survey by the Pew Research Center found that more than a third of Millennials have admitted to using numeric text shortcuts. The symbols used in this type of communication may be more intuitively interpreted by other generations, but have the same annoying effect upon them. This form of SMS text takes the form of visual depictions through an amalgamation of keyboard symbols that display an emotion. The most commonly used symbol :) is used to convey to a smile, often after a text message. Another common symbol ;) is used flirtatiously to signify a wink.

Although these aforementioned numeric codes and emotive symbols are common, SMS English predominantly occurs in the form of an abbreviated text message. From its humble beginnings that were limited to some cell phone providers, SMS is now the most widely used mobile-data service in the world. However, what may seem instinctive to the Millennials can appear encrypted to the older associates within the workplace that did not grow up with this experience. To that end, the following is a sample list of SMS text that may appear in the workplace with a deciphered translation for a non-Millennial's benefit:

Text	Translation
AATK.	Always at the keyboard
ACD	Alt Control Delete
ADAD	Another day another dollar
AEAP.	As early as possible
AFC.	Away from computer
AFIAA	As far as I am aware
BAK.	Back at keyboard
BM&Y.	Between me and you
BRB.	Be right back
CLM	Career-limiting move
COB	Close of Business
DNC	Does not compute
EOM	End of message
FBM	Fine by me
FOMC.	Falling off my chair
GBTW.	Get back to work
GGN	Got to go now
GIGO	Garbage in garbage out
GOI.	Get over it
IB.	I'm back
IDK	I don't know
IM	Instant Message
JK	Just kidding
NBD	No big deal
RME	Rolling my eyes
TKOY	Take care of yourself
TMI.	Too much information
TTYL.	Talk to you later
WU?	What's up?
XLNT	Excellent
YW	You are welcome

While some leaders may question whether this method of communication belongs in a professional setting, the reality is that it is now an integral part of the workplace due, in large part, to Millennial associates who brought it with them from their personal lives. Thus, despite evidence that suggests the Millennial generation recognizes that SMS is not appropriate in a professional environment, this vernacular has become far too infused in their DNA to cease all together. Consequently, the office communication paradigm has evolved in this new digital age much to the dismay of older generations in the workplace.

Moreover, SMS is not just used in these acronymic phrases, but is now utilized in full-blown sentences. For instance, the following is an instant message from a Millennial: "#s look gd…lnch @ 1 / back l8r." For Millennial associates, this is shorthand for, "The numbers look good. I am leaving for lunch at 1 p.m. and I will be back later." For non-Millennial associates, this message may appear to be written in a foreign language. Thus, while there are clear benefits for an organizational leader to get familiar with these new terms in order to more effectively engage with their Millennial associates, it is important to remember this should not involve modifying the way organizational leaders speak or integrate this language in their dialect. In fact, this may actually annoy the Millennials.

Conversely, it may be in the best interest of organizational leaders to demonstrate flexibility in their degree of *patience* with their Millennial associates as it relates to their communication policy. For instance, if an organization considers it unacceptable to send text messages during meetings, the organization should notify their Millennial associates of the policy in a collegial discussion and *not* presume they know it is improper decorum. This act of patience does not imply that they should allow them to breach their company policy. Rather, it suggests being sensitive to the Millennials that may view it as normal.

Understanding your Millennial associates' perspective can not only go a long way toward more effectively managing them in the workplace, but it can also begin to build a bridge toward earning their trust. This topic will be discussed in more detail in Chapter Nine. Thus, although SMS communication may appear a bit juvenile or self-indulgent to older generations, it becomes clear when you understand Millennials that it can be quite practical. Text-speak is more than just abbreviating and phonetic spelling to Millennials. It is focused on their drive to be very efficient and priority minded. In other words, they are abandoning grammar, syntax and convention in favor of expediency and accessibility.

The efficiency and succinctness of SMS communication is greatly valued by this younger generation that works well in a world of shorter attention spans, multitasking and social networks. From their cultural lens, it is considered very disrespectful to clutter text messages with content that is irrelevant to many recipients. Hence, the emergence of this new language (i.e. SMS) stemmed from the rise in real-time, text-based communications, such as Facebook, Twitter, instant messaging, e-mail, Internet, discussion boards/blogs, and mobile phone text messaging. Consequently, once organizational leaders understand the Millennial's perspective on this issue, they can start to recognize the practicality and value of an SMS communication style that is now being infused into Corporate America.

Additionally, it would behoove an organizational leader to avoid an over reliance on interoffice memos or snail mail letters for essential communication when it relates to this younger generation. This is primarily due to Millennials propensity toward real-time responsiveness. The Millennial survey results referenced in the introduction also suggest that organizational leaders should not expect instant replies to e-mail or a call back from a lengthy a voice mail due to a Millennial's preference for direct, instant communication.

Likewise, for Millennial associates, it is vital for them to be careful of the harmful implications SMS communication may have in a professional environment. Specifically, it can be confusing to the older generations that may not understand it. In addition, it can create a negative impression of them in a formal communication, such as business e-mail. Thus, Millennials could try to enhance their communication effectiveness by being more cautious, politically aware, and sensitive to the way in which they respond to colleagues.

In addition to taking the time to consider how the other generations will respond to the language they use in the workplace, Millennials need to address the fundamental challenge they face with the abundance of asynchronous technological devices they use, which is the limited *impact* they have in communications. While technology has clearly opened the door to new opportunities, particularly for the Millennial generation, one of its fundamental shortfalls is its inability to visually and verbally engage with colleagues.

The key elements of communication were studied in depth by Prof. Mehrabian at UCLA, where he concluded that the impact of communication is broken down as follows:

- 55% of impact is determined by body language (i.e. posture, gesture, eye contact),
- 38% by the tone of voice, and
- 7% by the content, that is, the "words" spoken.

  Ironically, the words have the least impact while the body language and tone of voice have the greatest impact, which speak to the importance of synchronous communication.

Consequently, when the language transmitted by the Millennials is limited to an asynchronous style of communication, it significantly limits their ability to emotionally connect with their colleagues. Hence, it is imperative for Millennials to utilize means of communication that allow their message to transmit synchronously for maximum impact.

As the English writer Robert Louis Stephenson said, "man is a creature that lives not upon bread alone, but primarily by catchwords." To that end, he understood that our use of language on a daily basis, particularly the use of casual and informal words, helps human beings to better understand their own world. Thus, through the utilization of our daily language, we relate to the world around us, as well as to each other. Consequently, by understanding the way which other generations communicate, organizational leaders can become more effective at empathizing and engaging with their Millennial associates.

Millennials should recall how *disconnected* it felt when their colleagues spoke to them in language they were not familiar with because they were new in the organization. Hence, Millennials should keep this in mind when using generational slang around elder colleagues at work. Nobody likes that feeling. Thus, it is everyone's responsibility to use common language to bridge the "communication gap" in a multi-generational workforce.

Chapter Four

The Significance of Technology

"One in three college students and young professionals from the Millennial generation consider the Internet to be as essential as resources like air, water, food and shelter."

This profound quote resulted from an international workforce study conducted by Cisco Systems in 2011. It depicts how steeped the Millennial generation is in technology. For better or worse, Millennials treat their multi-tasking hand-held gadgets almost like a body part. For instance, according to Pew Research, more than eight-in-ten say they sleep with a cell phone glowing by the bed, poised to disgorge texts, phone calls, emails, songs, news, videos, games and wake-up jingles. However, this convenience can, at times, yield to temptation with nearly two-thirds of Millennials admitting to texting while they drive.

Since birth, the Millennial generation has been immersed in technology. For this reason, they are often referred to as "digital natives" which is an expression that portrays them as individuals who can not recall a time in their life without the Internet, as well as rapid technological advancement. With the exception of the very oldest segment of this generation, Millennials do not recall the emergence of the Internet. Thus, for practically all of them, the Internet has always been an integral part of their life and cultural ethos.

This factor is one of the primary reasons that Millennials consider themselves to be the "always connected" generation. For the Baby Boomer generation, virtually all of the technological advancements we use today have evolved in their working years, which has given them a deep appreciation for their benefit. For Gen X, they grew up embracing most of today's technological advancements, including the ability to go online. However, Millennials do not go online. They are always online, which is the origin of this moniker. Hence, it is critical to understand the significant role the Internet has played in their lives.

Without growing up in this digital world, it can be difficult for other generations to truly grasp how fundamental technology is to Millennials. Not only do they use it for entertainment, communication and convenience, but also as a means for self expression and identification. This became very evident with Millennials in a Pew Research survey when asked what truly makes their generation unique. The overwhelming most common response was technology. In this cross generational study, some of the other distinctions that were identified by Millennials were pop culture, liberalism, intelligence and clothes.

A comparison of how their responses stacked up to the other three working generations are detailed below. While Gen X also identified with technology, the other two did not.

What Makes Your Generation Unique?

	Millennials	Gen X	Boomers	Silent
1.	Technology use (24%)	Technology use (12%)	Work ethic (17%)	WW II, Depression (14%)
2.	Music/Pop culture (11%)	Work ethic (11%)	Respectful (14%)	Smarter (13%)
3.	Liberal/Tolerant (7%)	Conservative/Trad'l (7%)	Values/Morals (8%)	Honest (12%)
4.	Smarter (6%)	Smarter (6%)	"Baby Boomers" (6%)	Values/Morals (10%)
5.	Clothes (5%)	Respectful (5%)	Smarter (5%)	Work ethic (10%)

Note: Based on respondents who said their generation was unique/distinct. Items represent individual, open-ended responses. Top five responses are shown for each age group. Sample sizes for sub-groups are as follows: Millennials, n=527; Gen X, n=173; Boomers, n=283; Silent, n=205.

The responses to this open-ended survey coalesce around certain general themes. For instance, Boomers and members of the Silent generation were prone to point to their differences between generations and point to historical experiences to defend distinctions. where as Millennials and Gen Xers were more likely to distinguish their generation by a lifestyle and defining characteristic, particularly technology use. It was also interesting to note that work ethic was identified by each generation with the exception of Millennials. Nevertheless, Millennials not prioritizing "work ethic" should not be confused with "an unwillingness to work hard," as will be explored in greater detail in Chapter Seven.

Technological and generational change often go hand in hand. That has certainly been the case for Millennials with their embrace for digital innovations. Over the past 15 years, the Internet and mobile phones have been widely adopted with Millennials *leading* the way as technology enthusiasts in America. The contributions that the Millennials are making to American culture and business methods is evident by the significant growth in technology adoption by non-Millennials since 2010 (as illustrated in the following chart).

Millennials lead on some technology adoption measures, but Boomers and Gen Xers are also heavy adopters

% of U.S. adults in each generation who say they ...

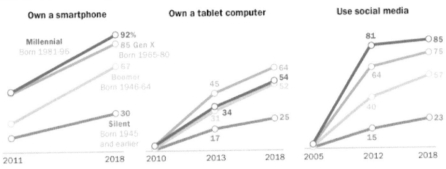

Source: Survey conducted Jan. 3-10, 2018. Trend data are from previous Pew Research Center surveys.

PEW RESEARCH CENTER

In order to get at the heart of this matter, it is key to understand the various views of technology from a generational perspective. In other words, although it is beneficial to get a clear understanding of *why* Millennials have embraced technological advancements, it is equally necessary to discern how the older generations have accepted it. To that end, we need to consider whether they feel it has made life easy or more complicated, brought people together or made them more isolated, led to more productive associates or caused them to waste time. These questions are particularly critical to consider in the workplace.

Recent Pew Research suggests an encouraging answer to this question. Note Pew surveyed each generation as to "whether the Internet was mostly a good thing," and the results are seen in the table below. Although every generation gave higher marks for the benefit the Internet had been to them personally as opposed to society as a whole, even the Silent generation overwhelmingly asserted a personal benefit. The lower "societal" marks each generation gave might be owing to concerns like lost privacy and time lost that was previously spent in conversation and other inter-personal pursuits. Chapter Twelve, "Leading a Multi-Generational Workforce," suggests that lessening the degree of this downside is a priority each generation in the workforce supports.

Older internet users less likely to view the internet as a positive for society

% of U.S. internet users who say the internet had mostly been a good thing for ...

	Society	You
Millennial Ages 22-37	73%	90%
Gen X Ages 38-53	69	89
Boomer Ages 54-72	68	89
Silent Ages 73+	63	78

60   80   100

Note: Include responses from internet users only.
Source: Survey conducted Jan. 3-10, 2018.

PEW RESEARCH CENTER

The recent gains by Non-Millennials notwithstanding, Millennials remain the generational leaders in comfort with technology and willingness to promptly explore new developments. Marc Prensky, an internationally acclaimed speaker, writer and consultant in education and learning, attributes the divergence to their technology acclimation. In his research, he draws a distinction between digital natives (i.e. the Millennials) and digital immigrants (i.e. all previous generations). Digital natives have always had technology as a huge part of their world where as digital immigrants have had to *learn* how to integrate it into their lives. Thus, as with anyone who learns a second language, digital immigrants will always retain their accent (i.e., foot in the past), which can make it more challenging to adapt because technology is not second nature to them (like it is for the digital natives).

A powerful example that illustrates this salient point is the simple task of reading a document on your computer. A digital native grew up viewing this effort as "mundane" where as a digital immigrant, particularly one who grew up in a non-computer era like the Silent generation, will resist this method and print it on paper instead. Thus, as Prensky's research indicates, it is not uncommon for a digital immigrant to naturally revert back to their first language (i.e. the way they initially learned to do something). Hence, it should be of no surprise that the Silent generation does not view technological advancements as fondly as the Millennials that were acclimated to it (as digital natives) in their upbringing. Examples of recent technology-related comfort level divergence between Millennials and earlier generations are seen in the display below.

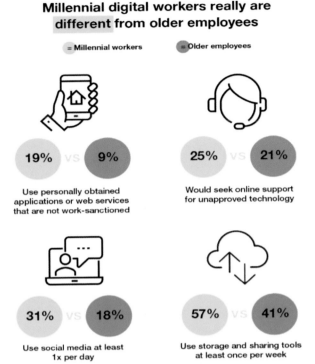

Millennial digital workers really are different from older employees

= Millennial workers = Older employees

| 19% vs 9% | 25% vs 21% |

Use personally obtained applications or web services that are not work-sanctioned

Would seek online support for unapproved technology

| 31% vs 18% | 57% vs 41% |

Use social media at least 1x per day

Use storage and sharing tools at least once per week

Another glaring technological distinction between generations is in Internet usage, both in frequency and in how it is accessed. The research highlighted in the chart below shows the Silent generation still may not use the Internet much besides a "daily checking of e-mails," but the younger generations continue to ramp up their frequency. Thus, this ramping up is partly due to the emerging new ways in which the Internet can be accessed, as indicated by the second of the two charts below. The reasons for this divergence are analogous to the Prensky's research. Hence, it is clear that our generational cultural lens plays an integral part in what we will do naturally and will manifestly influence our propensity toward technology. Consequently, these findings must play a role in forming our strategy to mitigate the generational differences. To the degree that these new ways promote business efficiency, Millennials will be able to lend a particular helping hand, while also needing to be patient and supportive of their "non-digital natives" colleagues.

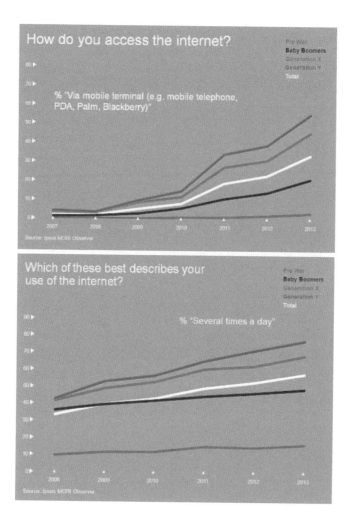

The impact on Millennials from these rapid technological advancements are vast, specifically in how they communicate with regard to speed and quality of language. The prior generations learned their language and communication style from parents, teachers and friends. However, Millennials learned their technical jargon, colloquialisms and chat language from the digital age in which they were raised. Millennials will often say "Mom and Dad may have taught me my first words, but technology taught me how to speak." Hence, the psychological impact from the technological advancements that Millennials have been exposed to have greatly shaped the vernacular they use. Some examples of the technology influences on communication by generation in the workforce are as follows.

Silent:	Rotary telephones, in-person communication and meetings
Boomer:	Touch-tone telephones, use of memos, networking meetings
Gen X:	Cell phones, phone conferences, e-mail, computer meetings
Millennial:	Smart phones, social networking, webcams, text messages

Another impact of growing up with technology plugged in 24/7 is the Millennials' preference for communication through e-mail and text messaging rather than face-to-face contact. Moreover, they also prefer webinars and online technology to traditional lecture-based presentations. Interestingly, although e-mails have been part of the culture since the early 1990s, they have not lost material relevance, with Gallup finding an average of 205 billion worldwide being sent daily, an average of 29 per person. Millennials still find e-mail useful due to its unlimited number of available characters, and the important but not urgent manner in which e-mails are typically received. The same 2014 Gallup survey found the following communication form preference differences by generation:

Use of Communication Devices Among Americans, by Age
% Who did this "a lot" the previous day
Sorted by % among 18- to 29-year-olds

	18 to 29	30 to 49	50 to 64	65+
	%	%	%	%
Send or read a text message	68	47	26	8
Make or receive a phone call using a cellphone	50	41	40	18
Send or read an email message	47	44	38	16
Post or read messages on Facebook, Instagram or some other social media site	38	20	17	6
Use Twitter, including posting or reading tweets	14	3	2	0
Make or receive a phone call using a business landline phone	13	19	15	8
Make or receive a phone call using a home landline phone	7	6	10	17

Sept 9-10, 2014

GALLUP

However, according to the aforementioned survey referenced in the introduction of this book, they strongly prefer face-to-face conversations when it comes to receiving feedback and performance appraisals from their managers. Hence, although their proclivity for asynchronous communication is evident, it does not translate for more important conversations that require the ability to observe body language and vocal tone.

An additional consideration that has evolved from these technological advances is the work-life balance. With digital devices hooked to the hip of Millennials, they are now connected to communication 24 hours a day. Consequently, the lines between their work life and personal life have *blurred*. In other words, because they are "always connected," they are likely to respond to messages at all hours of the day. Thus, they have inherently removed traditional work hours from their professional life. The impact to their employer is an associate that is reachable at any time during the day or night. However, this could cause an issue for employers with associates that are not exempt from earning overtime.

With the evolving increase in means of communication, Millennials have started to demand multiple channels (from their employer) as a mechanism to have an amplified voice with customers and colleagues. Essentially, they are insisting on having numerous tools at their disposal for multifaceted communication as illustrated in this chart below.

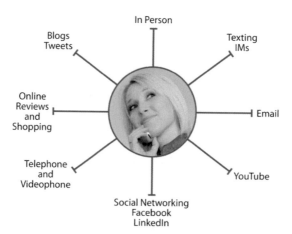

Quite a few organizations have conducted surveys to further investigate the ways in which Millennials will impact the workplace. Some of the more prominent and useful research came from the Pew Research Center, Pricewater-houseCoopers (PwC), KPMG, Johnson Controls, Deloitte, Brill Street and The Ethics Resource Center (ERC). In order to compare and contrast the Millennials comprehensively with five distinct characteristics from their generation, the summary of surveys below streamlines their ultimate findings.

Survey	How Generation Defined	Technology Participation	Diversity	Social Responsibility	Work-Life Balance
Pew Research	Born after 1980	88% text; 75% social networking; 59% Internet as source of news	Most racially tolerant, most diverse generation	Strong moral responsibility	Balanced work ethic
PwC	Entered workforce after 2000	92% are members of an online social network	80% would like to work abroad and most expect to use other languages	88% would choose employers whose social responsibility values reflect their own	66% expect to work regular hours with some flexibility
KPMG	Born June 1976–June 1991	Driven by new technology	Global perspective	Social conscience; volunteering appeals to sense of making a contribution to the greater good	Demand a more balanced mix between work, family, and outside interests
Johnson Controls	Born 1981–1993	Tech-savvy and will bring transformational technological solutions to the world	38% identify as non-white. Inclusive and community minded	96% want an environmentally aware workplace	56% prefer to work flexibly and choose when to work
Deloitte	Born 1982–1995	Tech-savvy and connected 24/7	Inclusive	47% value company culture and reputation	63% favor opportunities for growth and development over security; 23% favor flexible work hours
Brill Street	28 years and younger	77%–79% want remote work options and real-time feedback	87% influenced by acceptance of individuality	84% influenced by socially responsible business practices; 53% want a day off to volunteer	92% prefer flexible working hours
ERC	Born after 1980	Grew up with e-mail, Internet, cell phones, and immediate access to information; excellent at integrating technology into workplace	Attuned to and appreciative of diversity; connect easily with a greater diversity of races, religions, and sexual orientations	More likely to observe misconduct of other employees; value privacy less; information is to be shared rather than owned	Believe that doing a good job is about the work you do, not how many hours you put in

Source: *Bannon, Shele, Kelly Ford, and Linda Meltzer. 2011. Understanding Millennials in the Workplace. CPA Journal 81, no. 11: 61-65.*

As indicated in the preceding exhibit and previously referenced studies, it is clear that Millennials expect employers to have solid technology platforms that provide access through mobile devices. *Forbes* notes the "2016 Adobe Future of Work Report" reported that 81 percent of workers found that state-of-the-are technology as more important than office design or amenities and that 26 percent the sophistication of technology believed technology at their company is "ahead of the curve." *Forbes* also notes a "Radius Global Market Research" study on the adverse impact of office connectivity issues, for which 45 percent of employees reported increased stress, 41 percent asserted assistance to customers is frustrated, 36 percent said productivity is lowered and 77 percent say profits are lowered. The Adobe report also found a strong connection between the perceived quality of technology and employee morale, as presented below.

Feelings About Primary Job
Among U.S. Office Workers that See Own Company to be "Ahead of the Curve" vs. "Behind the Times" – Showing Top 2 Box

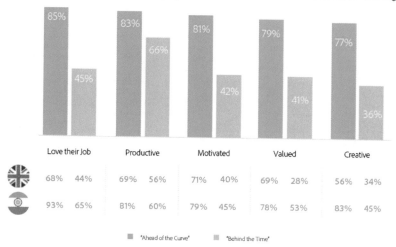

As a matter of fact, the majority of Millennials surveyed in New Generation Workers' study indicated that state-of-the-art technology was one of the most important considerations in selecting an employer; however, more than 20 percent of respondents that had a job thought their current employer's technology was not sufficient.

In the survey that was conducted for this book (referenced in the Introduction), the results strongly indicated that Millennials have a fierce expectation for organizations to equip them with modern technology. For instance, when Millennials were asked "How can your current employer improve to meet the needs your generation?" by a significant margin they mentioned "technology" more often than any other response, particularly in the private sector where budgets are more robust. In one of the multiple choice questions, "If my employer does not provide me the most up-to-date technology, I will likely go to one that does," only 26.6 percent of Millennials *disagreed* with this statement. Hence, it would behoove organizations to heed this overt call for technology from both a recruiting perspective and for retention considerations to satisfy their Millennials' expectations.

Given the significance of technology to Millennials in the workplace, what could an organization do to protect itself against a Millennial exodus when the economy recovers and competition is back in full force vying for this next generation of leaders? Based on a study conducted by The Gartner Group, the most notable and strategic need is "virtualization," which eliminates duplicate copies of data on real storage devises with cloud computing. From a personnel perspective, a much appreciated Millennial addition would be a virtual class available online (or downloadable) for suitable associate training.

Another common request of Millennials for their employer is to "loosen up" their technology policy. This was a universal response from Millennials in the aforementioned survey in all sectors. In fact, those exact words "loosen up" were mentioned a significant number of times throughout the survey, second only to technology when asked what else can your employer do to enhance your environment in the workplace. Having said that, it is also clear that no organization is going to permit their associates to logon to Facebook when they are on the clock. Moreover, it is important for Millennial associates to realize that some industries have regulatory limitations that preclude them from accessing certain websites, particularly social media. Thus, how can an organization avoid the perception that they are too rigid while complying with their corporate policy and supervision rules?

First and foremost, organizational leaders must proactively discuss the regulatory policy that they must abide by to remain compliant with their associates (Millennials and otherwise). This transparency will go a long way toward helping Millennials understand that it is not the company's rigidity causing this policy, but rather a governmental agency that has oversight in their industry. As an example, securities-licensed sales associates are not permitted to list their employer on their Facebook page without extensive supervision that will assure a solicitation is not taking place in a manner that is prohibited by the law.

Aside from legal requirements, organizations should challenge themselves to find creative ways to quench a Millennials' thirst for technology, such as the Internet, without compromising their core values. One option that has been well received by Millennials is an open computer area located on a convenient floor that provides them open access (with some exceptions of course) to surf the Internet on their breaks and lunch. This alternative could also mitigate Millennials from using their smart phones to satisfy this strong desire.

It could also be advantageous for organizational leaders to consider establishing a technology committee with Millennial representation to examine opportunities to open up their policy. This approach would allow Millennials to feel that their voice is being heard, rather than simply dismissed. Ultimately, this would allow an organization to vet various ideas in an inclusive forum that would be attractive to the "always connected" generation while balancing this phenomenon with the businesses need to be productive and efficient.

To some organizational leaders, this approach may seem like they are acquiescing to the demands of this impending generation. However, bear in mind that a major benefit from retaining and attracting them into your workforce can be a competitive advantage. The key is to design the technology committee in a manner that provides the organization benefit as well. For instance, rather than just charging them to examine suitable standards for technology use, leaders could commission Millennials to redesign the workplace in a manner that releases their innovative potential. Given this generation's insatiable appetite to maximize technology, natural ability to multi-task and intrinsic desire to collaborate, they will be well positioned to team up with the organizational leaders to unleash their talents in a profitable manner. Apple, Inc. is a company that has personified this model.

For Millennial associates, it is imperative that they embrace this opportunity with "Level 5" leadership, which Jim Collins defines as "putting the organization's interests before your own." Conversely, if Millennial efforts become self-serving, it will defeat the purpose of such a committee. Thus, it is essential that they constantly remind themselves of the mission and core values they should be espousing in order to demonstrate they are up to the task. For instance, Millennials need to be cognitive of the expense requirement and risk budget that's deemed acceptable by the organization and regulatory implications.

In close, how can an organization avoid the devastating label that their technology is "obsolete" or their policies therein are considered "too rigid" for Millennials? In highly regulated industries, such as financial services, it is will be challenging for organizations to get sufficiently comfortable with social media given the oversight that is required. However, is there a device that permits an organization to restrict access to undesirable applications and yet provide the necessary encrypted security to use it in their business? The answer is yes. The Apple iPad has proven able to satisfy both directives. It has the power to bestow access to news outlets, the Internet and digital technology more efficiently than most other devices, while imparting security to organizations via providers such as Good Technology. Thus, a company-issued iPad device could be a good starting point to offer to tech-savvy associates that travel (as a replacement for their laptop) and to satisfy their digital appetite.

Chapter Five

The Emergence of Social Media

"Social Media is about sociology and psychology more than technology."

This quote by Brian Solis, principal at Altimeter Group and host of the web show *Revolution*, epitomizes why social media has its own chapter in this book. When properly understood, it is evident that social media is multi-faceted, and thus should not be limited to a mere subset of the prior chapter on technology. Nonetheless, it is important to bear in mind that technological devices, such as smartphones, are the means people use to access social media. However, the impetus for social media is much more complicated. From a sociological viewpoint, Millennials have shown to have a tremendous propensity to use social media as a "teamwork" mechanism to stay informed of others' opinions. Although they certainly prefer to be identified as individuals, this should not be confused with their desire to work in groups in order to make decisions more judiciously.

Psychologically, the Millennial generation's mind has embraced social media out of their proclivity for self expression. Social media has become an excellent complement for Millennials to amalgamate technology with their instinctive desire to socially network with others of like mind. Thus, social media is about relationships rather than technology. Likewise, social media has become a tool that enables Millennials to have a voice in all parts of their life, which is an expectation of this generation (as depicted in Chapter One).

Thus, this inherent desire to engage with others, toss around ideas, share feedback and build relationships has played a fundamental role in the development of this enduring trait that lends itself to the role social media can fill. With technology serving as the great facilitator, it is clear that social media is not just a fad that will diminish in the near term, but rather is a new way of communicating that is here to stay, particularly for Millennials.

So when did social media emerge to become the ubiquitous medium it is today? It started out in the form of generalized online communities, such as Geocities, Tripod.com and Theglobe.com, in the mid-1990s. However, 10 years later, it still only amounted to a mere 5 percent of public use. It really did not become mainstream until 2008 when candidate Barack Obama used it to catapult himself into the office of President. Through a variety of social networking applications under the banner of a movement, the Obama campaign created an unprecedented force to raise money, organize locally and get out the vote that helped it topple the Clinton machine and subsequently John McCain.

Thus, regardless of your view on politics, it is undeniable the significant role that social media played in energizing the Obama presidential campaign through a grass roots effort that propelled a virtual unknown (two years before) to the most powerful position of leadership in the world. It is also important to note that a key demographic that this social media campaign was targeting was the Millennial generation, which played a prominent role in his election. Since this election, and continuing into the last five years as well, the popularity of social media amongst Americans and organizations therein has grown expeditiously. Using social media network leader Facebook as a surrogate for interest in social media more broadly, Silent Generation interest in social media is growing slowly but surely, while Boomer and Gen X interest is growing rapidly, and Millennial interest is holding at its already high level. One reason why Facebook use is not approaching 100% percent among Millennials is the emergence of other networks, as indicated in the following charts.

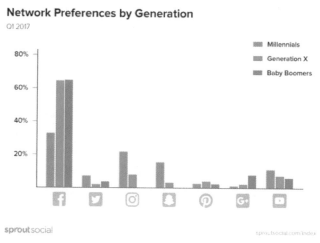

Network Preferences by Generation

Q1 2017

sproutsocial

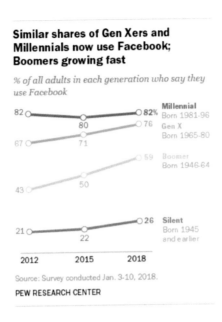

Similar shares of Gen Xers and Millennials now use Facebook; Boomers growing fast

% of all adults in each generation who say they use Facebook

Pew Research finds that 69 percent of adults overall use social networking sites, with 94 percent of Millennials using them. This generational divergence should be of no surprise considering their upbringing and cultural lens. It is a recurrent characteristic that the Millennials have identified with in their personal lives, as well as in their workplace.

If you are not sure what is meant by social media, you are not likely a Millennial. Essentially, there are six distinct types of social media today: Collaborative Projects (e.g., Wikipedia), Social Networking Sites (e.g., Facebook, Instagram, LinkedIn), Blogs (e.g., Twitter), Content Communities (e.g., You Tube), Virtual Game Worlds (e.g., World of Warcraft, Fortnite) and Virtual Social Worlds (e.g., Second Life). The most prevalent of these categories are the Social Networking sites, which in effect group people into specific factions online (such as a small rural community or neighborhood subdivision).

Of the aforementioned social networking sites, the most popular is Facebook. For 2018, Zephoria estimates Facebook had 2.23 million unique visitors per month. Content Community site You Tube is second, at 1.9 billion, and fellow Social Networking site Instagram is third at one billion. Facebook's May 19, 2012 initial public offering generated $16 billion, more than three times the estimate made in its Securities and Exchange Commission

(SEC) filing just three months before. So what application does this have for organizations? For one, recruiting the top talent. Major corporations from a variety of industries, such as KPMG, General Electric and Verizon, are using a soft-sell approach on Facebook to entice, but not offend, the Millennial prospects to pursue their employment. These firms are being very cautious not to send a message that may cause resentment or rejection from an improper intrusion on their personal life. Moreover, these businesses have also enlisted their own associates to engage a top prospect. Although it is too soon to deem this tactic viable, it has had some success in these particular situations.

An example of an early adopter of Facebook for recruiting Millennials was Ernst & Young (E&Y), which established a prospecting website in 2006. However, unlike the previous examples, they used a more direct approach. They explicitly state, "*We are not interested in seeing your profiles. It's not that we are not interested in you. We respect your privacy and understand that you use Facebook to socialize with your friends.*" E&Y does this to alleviate any fears that they are on Facebook to spy on anyone's profile. To attract people to their page, particularly Millennials, they update their page weekly with new content and pictures. However, the most provocative part of their page is the Wall, which allows all visitors to post comments about E&Y. Although this tactic may allow them to ingratiate themselves with the firm, it also opens the organization up to criticism. Believe it or not, E&Y seems comfortable with this risk and doesn't remove pejorative comments from the Wall with the exception of vulgarity. Ultimately, although E&Y attracts tens of thousands of Millennials to their page while hiring some, they treat it more like it is a branding tool.

From a business perspective, the most widely used social network is LinkedIn. It is the third most popular in the overall ranking, but has more business applications than any other type of social media. Moreover, it has proven to be an effective tool to promote an organization's brand exposure, as well as demonstrate their professional prowess to employment prospects in a cost efficient manner. Some other LinkedIn applications are:

- Networking – connect with people in the same industry or area of expertise
- Improve your Internet ranking – very high page ranking on Google search
- Enhance your search engine results – drive traffic to organization's website

- Reference Checks – perform blind, reverse and company reference checks
- Increase Job Search Relevancy – ability to search for specialized expertise

For Millennials, this list of business applications should heed a sage notice to you: Update and clean up your social networking pages before you apply for a position. Moreover, given the aforementioned impact that can result from social media networks, Millennials and organizations should take every precaution to protect their reputation on the Internet. Jeff Bezos, the CEO at Amazon.com, emphatically makes this point with the following quote, "*If you make customers unhappy in the physical world, they might each tell six friends. However, if you make customers unhappy on the Internet, they can each tell six thousand friends.*" Thus, it is absolutely imperative to assure your reputation does not become tarnished on social media for fear it could go "viral" (i.e., computer term for spreading rapidly across the Internet and garnering negative attention in a short period).

This is particularly true for the Millennial generation. A blind purchase is not the norm with this group, nor is relying on one person's opinion to make a purchase decision unless that particular person carries significant influence. This is largely due to the instant gratification they receive from always being connected and their deep desire to research their purchases in advance. This is not only true for products, but for employers as well. They appear to have no issue receiving reviews from complete strangers so long as they are detailed enough and can identify a positive or negative trend. As a matter of fact, this strategy of digitally reviewing products and people has been the Millennial generation's modus operandi since a very young age, with the average beginning at age seven or eight.

Like online purchases, Millennials will shop employers through social media by obtaining feedback from others. Hence, this should also serve as a call to organizational leaders to assure what is written about their firm online is accurate. Bear in mind that just as leaders check the candidate's background, candidates will vet the organization as well.

The following four charts provide astute insights as to generational social network use practices, which are no longer dominated by Millennials yet for which Millennials remain the trendsetters. With regard to Millennials, Facebook now has more competition from other social networks than previously. However, Facebook remains dominant in the frequency of visits. The many different daily media options Millennials have, and indeed actually utilize, are seen in the third chart below. And the recent "taking a break from Facebook" trend is seen in the fourth chart, which may reflect the all encompassing degree many have found Facebook to be, and which businesses may have to account for in their Facebook marketing efforts.

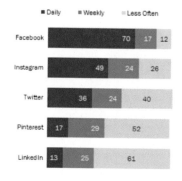

Frequency of social media site use

% of social media site users who use a particular site with the following frequencies (% is reported among each specific site's user groups, e.g., 70% of Facebook users use the site on a daily basis)

■ Daily   ■ Weekly   ■ Less Often

	Daily	Weekly	Less Often
Facebook	70	17	12
Instagram	49	24	26
Twitter	36	24	40
Pinterest	17	29	52
LinkedIn	13	25	61

Pew Research Center's Internet Project September Combined Omnibus Survey, September 11-14 & September 18-21, 2014. N=1,597 internet users ages 18+

PEW RESEARCH CENTER

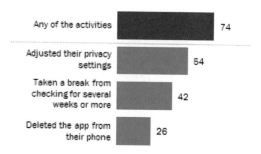

42% of Facebook users have taken a break from the site in the past year

% of U.S. adults who use Facebook who say they have done the following in the last 12 months ...

Any of the activities	74
Adjusted their privacy settings	54
Taken a break from checking for several weeks or more	42
Deleted the app from their phone	26

Note: Those who did not answer or gave other responses are not shown.
Source: Survey conducted May 29-June 11, 2018.

PEW RESEARCH CENTER

Millennials Rack Up 18 Hours of Media Use Per Day
Average time millennials in the U.S. spend interacting with media per day (hh:mm)*

03:34	03:12	02:19	01:47	01:47
Browse the internet	Social networking	Watch live TV	Play video games	Watch timeshifted TV

01:15	01:15	01:04	01:04	00:32
Go to the movies	Listen to the radio	Use email, text, texting apps	Talk about news/ products/brands	Read print magazines /newspapers

* media activities are not mutually exclusive, based on a 2014 survey among 839 U.S. adults aged 18-36

THE WALL STREET JOURNAL.   Source: Crowdtap, Ipsos MediaCT   **statista**

Social Media – Frequency of Usage by Millennials

Social network	Used daily	Used occassionally
Facebook	57%	31%
YouTube	29%	54%
Instagram	26%	23%
Twitter	13%	21%
Pinterest	10%	25%
Reddit	8%	15%
Tumblr	7%	14%

Source: American Press Institute. (2015). *How Millennials Use and Control Social Media.* Arlington, VA: American Press Institute.

As enticing as this growing trend may appear, it creates some fundamental risks that exist for organizations in industries that are highly regulated. For instance, the SEC has issued an edict warning financial advisors to be wary about using social media as has FINRA (Financial Industry Regulation Authority). Thus, financial services organizations need to be very cautious in approaching an ambiguous line that has not yet been defined.

In spite of these chilling admonitions from the feared regulators, many financial advisors continue to use social media in their marketing efforts, particularly Millennials. They are in dire need of a new prospecting technique since cold-calling has been rejected by the public by and large, and even deemed illegal in some states. To that end, social media has become an ideal substitute since affinity groups and networks can provide them with the ability to "connect" with people of similar interests that desire financial or investment advice from a trusted friend or contact. However, beyond the SEC and FINRA guidance, many additional "best practices" have been proposed in industry literature, including as seen in the 2017 *Forbes* article, "15 Tips to Used Social Media (Compliantly)". Five of the tips are as follows:

- Be fully cooperative with firm policy and consult compliance area with any questions
- Define areas of expertise to help clients succeed, and reflect personal brand as well, without straying into views on controversial subjects.
- Set up and use profiles compliantly using your e-mail address to aid in recordkeeping while avoid making recommendations and endorsements.
- Share useful content that has firm's compliance area advance approval, such as pre-approved libraries of articles or publications.
- Use social media research capabilities for prospecting.

Using guidance like this, financial advisor use of social media is thriving. Between 2011 and 2015, *InvestmentNews* found that financial advisor use of LinkedIn increased from 39 percent to 72 percent, Twitter use increased from 14 percent to 44 percent and Facebook use increased from 23 percent to 34 percent. The "2015 Putnam Investments Social Advisor Survey" has more specific findings on how particular investment advisor activities are accomplished using the three social networking sites.

Financial Advisors and Social Media

FINDINGS: BUSINESS GOALS

Advisors were asked how they are leveraging their primary social networks for business.	in	f	y
Improving my referral network	65%	54%	48%
Connecting with peers	59%	52%	56%
Enhancing current client relationships	54%	65%	49%
Building my brand identity	52%	57%	47%
Expanding my professional knowledge	45%	47%	51%
Promoting myself as a thought leader	41%	43%	51%

The 2015 Putnam Investments Survey of Financial Advisors' Use of Social Media was conducted in partnership with Brightwork Partners LLC among 817 advisors nationally who have been advising retail clients for at least two years. The online study was conducted in July 2015.

In addition to being a superb medium for financial advisors to service customers and prospect new clients, it can also be an effective mode for a small sales force to reach their clients using a hybrid or virtual wholesaling model.

Thus, for Millennial associates, it is clear that organizations (even in highly regulated industries) are starting to get more comfortable with social media. However, these associates will need to tread lightly when making a request of employers. In this environment, it is in their best interest to evaluate the risks before entering into new ventures. To that end, it would behoove Millennials to provide their organizations with research, rather than just demanding access to this new medium. For organizational leaders, it has become clear that social media is here to stay and should be viewed as an opportunity. Hence, a social media strategy has become vital.

With a voluminous amount of social media choices available on the Internet, how should an organization go about developing a strategy? The simple answer is to go where the customers are initially, while maintaining enough flexibility when the environment or trends warrant change. An efficient approach at the outset is to establish content from a central platform that can be repurposed and reformatted for distribution via a variety of mediums, which should include social networking sites, the company website or e-mail.

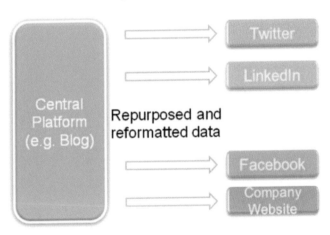

When selecting which social media sites to utilize, it is important to select those that are conducive for their customer's behavior, rather than what is popular today. For instance, many organizations dismissed Twitter several years ago when it was viewed as merely a personal tool in favor of the then-most-popular social network site, MySpace, and more recently were skeptical about the potential of Instagram. Now fast forward to today. Instagram's one billion visitors per month make it second to only Facebook in social networking site popularity. Twitter still remains popular with 336 million monthly visitors. And as for MySpace? It has long faded into effective irrelevance.

In summary, it is clear that organizational leaders from practically every industry need to develop a social media strategy to remain relevant in their business. Social media has emerged into a force that needs to be integrated into every organization's culture in a manner that maintains their values and fuels their mission, yet will adjust to the changing dynamics of their customer base. However, as they explore these powerful yet potentially disruptive opportunities, their business leaders will need to give earnest thought to "how" it will affect their business from a productivity standpoint, a generational perspective and a regulatory position. In other words, the expense needs to be weighed against the result, as well as the opportunity cost of those resources. Hence, although it is apparent that this medium can not be ignored, it should be employed and implemented in a thoughtful way.

Chapter Six

The Importance of Education

"If you think education is expensive, try ignorance."

This quote by Derek Bok, former president of Harvard University, personifies the Millennial generation's perspective regarding the importance they place on education. It becomes evident when examining their prominent enrollment in college between the ages of 18 to 24. According to a Pew Research study done early in the decade, the Millennials saw approximately 40 percent of their generation enrolled in college during this age span, which is a generational record high. In comparison, 24 percent of Baby Boomers and 33 percent of Gen X were enrolled in college during the same period of their life. In Pew's 2014 update of this study titled "The Rising Cost of Not Going to College," the research found the unemployment rate of college-educated persons versus non-college-educated was 3.8 percent versus 12.2 percent, respectively. The study also produced the chart below, which suggests that the stakes of attending versus not attending college are higher for Millennials than they were for older generations. Hence, this data not only shows the arrant importance of education among the vast majority of Millennials, but it should also serve as a "wake-up" call to organizations about the value potential employees will place on a company-sponsored tuition reimbursement and student loan repayment program.

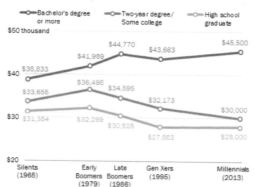

Rising Earnings Disparity Between Young Adults with And Without a College Degree

Median annual earnings among full-time workers ages 25 to 32, in 2012 dollars

Notes: Median annual earnings are based on earnings and work status during the calendar year prior to interview and limited to 25- to 32-year-olds who worked full time during the previous calendar year and reported positive earnings. "Full time" refers to those who usually worked at least 35 hours a week last year.

Source: Pew Research Center tabulations of the 2013, 1995, 1986, 1979 and 1965 March Current Population Survey (CPS) Integrated Public Use Micro Samples

PEW RESEARCH CENTER

This chapter will examine in great detail education and employment attributes of Millennials by analyzing the educational attainment of this generation and compare it to their older colleagues in the workforce. Moreover, it will analyze the working lives of Millennials, including their attitudes toward their vocation and career. One thing that is clear is that Millennials have become the most educated generation in American history, as Pew Research found when it revisited this issue in 2017.

Given this increased focus in education that is evident in Millennials, the question is: what was the impetus that initiated this paradigm shift with this generation? In order to get to the heart of this matter, it is important to recognize another vocational shift that had transpired with parents from the Silent generation. A new norm

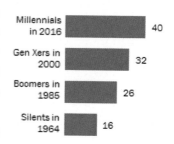

Young workers in U.S. more likely than ever to be college graduates

% of employed 25- to 29-year-olds with a bachelor's degree or more

Millennials in 2016	40
Gen Xers in 2000	32
Boomers in 1985	26
Silents in 1964	16

Note: "Employed" refers to those who were at work in the week prior to survey or who were temporarily absent from their jobs.

Source: Pew Research Center analysis of 1964, 1985, 2000 and 2016 Current Population Survey Annual Social and Economic Supplements (IPUMS).

PEW RESEARCH CENTER

had been established with both parents working, which essentially resulted in their kids returning to an empty home from school to fend for themselves. Ultimately, the effects from the *latchkey* environment caused great concern from many Boomer parents who felt this support system had failed the kids both at home and school. Consequently, when Boomer parents were at the helm, they began to revere, shelter and protect their kids. Moreover, many Boomer parents have placed additional pressure on their Millennial children by setting high standards, such as insisting on college prep classes. This strong achievement orientation espoused by Baby Boomers has shown to be especially true for Millennials in higher socioeconomic status.

During this same period, a national commission report on education was issued by the federal government warning the American public of widespread illiteracy, declines in standardized test scores, diluted curricula, and severe shortage of qualified teachers. This report, which was positioned as "an open letter to the American people" ardently depicted an educational system in crisis. This edict titled "A Nation at Risk" propelled educational policy into the national spotlight, sanctioned a heightened role for the federal government in the school systems, and galvanized two and a half decades of reforms ranging from the accountability movement to the "No Child Left Behind" Act passed by Congress in 2001. Hence, it was largely a combination of an over-protective government and over-protective parents that ultimately produced the Millennial mindset on the importance of higher education. Thus, these factors will continue to intensely affect their cultural lens.

The chart referenced in Chapter One illustrates that every Millennial demographic surpassed their 25 to 29 year old Gen X equivalent in bachelor degree attainment, with 46 percent versus 36 percent attainment for women, 36 percent versus 29 percent attainment for men, 65 percent versus 56 percent attainment for Asians, 47 percent versus 37 percent attainment for Whites, 27 percent versus 20 percent attainment for Blacks and 21 percent versus 11 percent attainment for Hispanics. Nevertheless, a recent downturn in age 18-24 college enrollment has emerged, with NCES data showing an increase from 38.8 percent to 42.1 percent from 2007 to 2011, but a decline from 42 percent to 40.5 percent in 2015. Despite their good intentions, what is ultimately holding some of these Millennials back? The Pew study cited in the introduction of this chapter found the most prevalent response to be a lack of money to pay for their college (36 percent), which is primarily attributed to the soaring cost of higher education. Another common reason cited by the Millennials was a lack of time. In fact, more than a third (35 percent) said it really just came down to not having enough time due to working in order to support themselves. In spite of this large percentage of Millennials that cited "work" as the reason they are not pursuing higher education, research has shown that nearly a quarter of Millennials work either part or full time while enrolled in school. However, it should be noted that (as it relates to employment), Millennials are considerably less likely to be working full time (61 percent) than Gen Xers (70 percent) due in large part to the stage they are at in life. Moreover, as illustrated in the following chart, Millennials are more likely to work part time (11 percent) as members of Gen X (9 percent) and Baby Boomers (10 percent). It should also be noted that part time includes both those who do so by choice (i.e., not working full time to make more time to attend college) and those who would prefer to work full time but are not able to find it. On the other hand, the number of Baby Boomers working full time being vastly below Gen Xers (40 percent versus 70 percent) is directly attributed to the large number of Baby Boomers who have already retired from work.

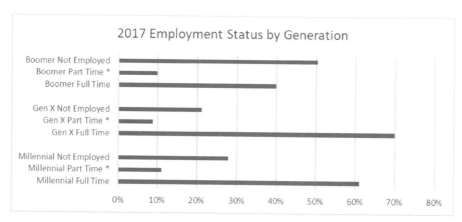

The present state of the economy has also influenced educational choices. Due to the 2008-2009 "Great Recession," many Millennials pursued additional education to gain better employment options once the economy recovered. This led to the percentage of Millennials who were fully employed being even lower than that directly caused by the bad economy. However, the stronger economy in the last few years likely has had the opposite effect, incenting greater interest in full time employment among Millennials, in part to make progress paying down significant loans many took earlier in the decade.

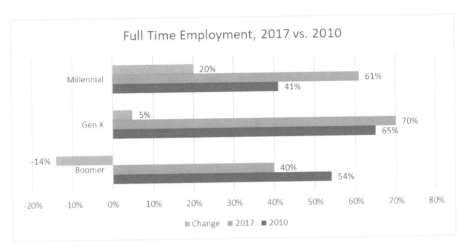

Even in the remnants of the poor economy from several years ago, the Millennials who pressed on with education can expect a pay-off once the economy recovered, as seen in 2017 surveys produced by Statista and Macrotrends below. This has been a timeless truth and proven benefit from an increase education for all generations past and present. As shown below, each level of education achievement has led to an increase in earnings.

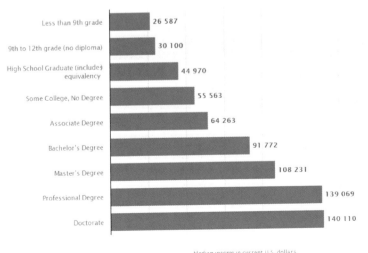

Higher education has consistently led to lower unemployment, as illustrated below.

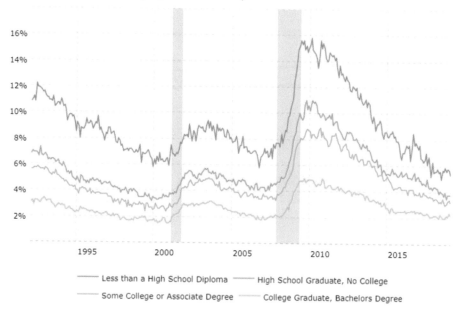

Unemployment Rate by Educational Level

However, an unintended consequence that resulted from the increased focus that has been placed on education is the enormous debt that Millennials have incurred from student loans. In 2014, the previously noted "The Rising Cost of Not Going to College" research notwithstanding, Pew found college graduates who needed to take loans to be at a major economic disadvantage. It found that the average college educated young adult had an average net worth of $64,700 if he or she carried no education debt, but had an average net worth of only $8,700 if loans were taken. This difference in net worth is much larger than the average college debt level of recent graduates ($13,000) because of much higher average incidence of *other debt* as well (i.e., mortgage, auto, credit card). In fact, Pew Research found the average total debt level of young adults with educational debt to be $137k, and only $73k for those without educational debt.

And another way to express this issue is comparing debt levels to annual income levels. Pew Research did so in 2014 as presented below.

Median Debt-to-Household-Income Ratio Much Higher for Student Debtors

Median total debt as % of household income, among young households

COLLEGE EDUCATED　　　　　　　　　　　**NOT COLLEGE EDUCATED**

Has student debt

108.3　　　181.2　　　190.7　　　　○ 204.6

　　　　　　　　138.5　　　127.1　　　○ 107.9

○　　No student debt

73.9

Has student debt

76.3　　94.5　　86.8　　　○ 100.2

No student debt

31.7　　27.5　　33.2　　　○ 10.2

2001　　2004　　2007　　2010　　2001　　2004　　2007　　2010

Note: Young households are households with heads younger than 40. Households are characterized based on the educational attainment of the household head. "College educated" refers to those with a bachelor's degree or more. Student debtor households have outstanding student loan balances or student loans in deferment. The debt-to-income ratio is tabulated for each household. The median ratio is reported. Households reporting zero income were reset to $1 of income in order to compute the ratio.

Source: Pew Research Center tabulations of the 2001 to 2010 Survey of Consumer Finances

PEW RESEARCH CENTER

Based on multiple surveys conducted by the College Board with this cohort, the majority of Millennials indicated their student loan debt will change their career plans and postpone life decisions, such as buying a home, getting married and having children.

This challenge for many Millennials could be an opportunity in disguise for some organizations that are willing to reconsider their employee retention programs. Currently, most large organizations offer their key associates some form of stock ownership or long-term retention incentive as a method to get them more involved in the firm's profitability and incent them to stay with the employer prospectively. Although these programs seem to achieve this objective for the older generations, Millennials have expressed negligible interest as a result of where they are in their career. However, given the aforementioned student loans they have accrued, an employee retention program that pays back a portion of their obligation for them would deliver a more immediate and valued carrot for them.

This type of program would not only appeal to them financially (by removing a burden that consumes them according to several empirical studies), but may ultimately serve as a *golden handcuff* that retains Millennials with an organization for the long run. For practitioners, the strategic question for organizations will be: Are Millennials going to be extensively different from

Boomers or Gen Xers when they reach middle age, and substantially distinct in such a way that organizations have to change the way they do business? For the most part, it is virtually impossible to know with certainty. However, some shifts are already evident and if they continue, they will require an adjustment for organizations. For instance, Millennials have much higher obesity rates and less overall fitness than Boomers and Gen Xers at the same age. According to a 2015 CDC/NCHS study, among Millennials and young Gen Xers the rate of obesity is estimated to exceed 30 percent. To compound this concern, Millennials are less likely to identify themselves as overweight according to these studies in comparison with earlier studies when people in this age group were appreciably less overweight than today.

Figure 1. Prevalence of obesity among adults aged 20 and over, by sex and age: United States, 2011–2014

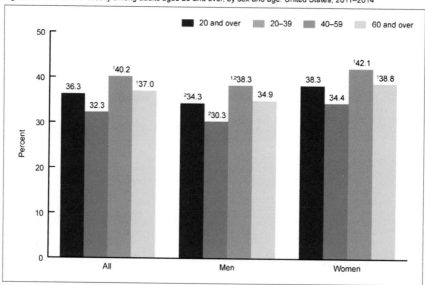

[1]Significantly different from those aged 20–39.
[2]Significantly different from women of the same age group.
NOTES: Totals were age-adjusted by the direct method to the 2000 U.S. census population using the age groups 20–39, 40–59, and 60 and over. Crude estimates are 36.5% for all, 34.5% for men, and 38.5% for women.
SOURCE: CDC/NCHS, National Health and Nutrition Examination Survey, 2011–2014.

If current health-related behaviors do not improve, it is reasonable to expect that Millennials will have noticeably substandard health as a result of obesity than did older cohorts at the same age. If obesity ultimately settles in at epidemic levels, organizations will likely experience an increase in illness-related absenteeism, increasing health costs from a growing unhealthy workforce and a decrease in productivity that goes along with an ill workforce. If this shift continues from a sedentary lifestyle and poor food choices, the Millennials ability to function as highly productive employees will be compromised.

Hence, to preempt this trend from continuing, it would behoove organizations to begin implementing health behavior change programs that help Millennials modify their life behavior. The long-term strategic consequences for employers of not assisting their associates to deal with this issue are substantially greater than the short-term investment necessary to promote this initiative. So what does this matter have to do with education?

A 2013 Statista study found that obesity rates among adults decreased at each level of higher education for each of the age groups they studied.

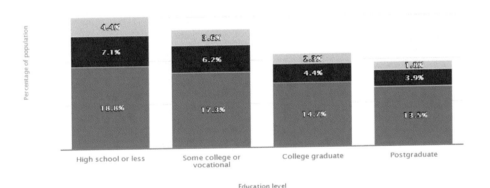

● Obese class I (BMI 30 to <35● Obese class II (BMI 35 to <40 ● Obese class III (BMI 40+)*

As illustrated in the prior chart, another approach organizations can use to address the obesity issue is to promote higher education through financial support. Thus, whether they institute a health improvement program in the workplace or espouse better living via education, organizations have the opportunity to help reverse this growing epidemic with innovative HR practices that incent behaviors. To that end, education has not only demonstrated the ability to propel Millennials into an organization better equipped to handle their business needs, but can promulgate improved health through higher learning.

Chapter Seven

Aligning Ethical Values

"They combine the teamwork ethic of the Boomers with the can-do attitude of the Silent Generation and the technological savvy of the Xers. At first glance, and even at second glance, Generation Next may be the ideal workforce—and ideal citizens."

This quote from the authors of *Generations at Work* portrays some of the positive attributes of the Millennial generation that are reflected in numerous books in the popular press today. Moreover, experience has also shown them to be proficient multitaskers and attuned to diversity in the workplace. However, negative traits have also been ascribed to Millennials, such as a lack of basic literacy fundamentals, very short attention spans, and disloyalty to their employer. As with any generation, there is always be a mixture of good and bad ethical values. So the real question is "how will the Millennials behave at work?"

Some generational theorists such as Jamie Notter argue that Millennials have their *own* ethical values and assumptions about workplace behavior. Likewise, research reports from various sources maintain that the Millennials do not hold the same set of ethical and professional standards as their predecessors. Conversely, scientific research by authors and educators such as Jennifer Deal (with the Center of Creative Leadership) contend that all generations have analogous values -- they just choose to express them differently.

Regardless whether one believes that the Millennial generation has distinct ethical values or not, it is apparent that gaps that exist within a multi-generational workforce can drive a wedge between your associates. Hence, many business leaders are wondering how they can ensure that the ethical values shared by their organization are properly *aligned* to avoid miscommunication, disarray, ineptitude, or worst of all – put their company at risk. The first step to addressing this challenge is to better understand the current generations.

It is important to recognize that each generation has been shaped by their cultural lens (i.e. events they have experienced during their formative years), demographic trends and national phenomena. Moreover, they come to work with a distinguishing set of skills and challenges that impact their organizations, and have the potential to help or thwart relationships with managers and coworkers. The following table depicts a portrait of key generations in the U.S. workforce, including its attributes and beliefs about work.

	Baby Boomers	Generation X	Millennials
Significant world events and cultural trends shaping their worldview	Born after end of World War II Raised in era of economic prosperity Assassinations of RFK, JFK, and MLK, Jr. Civil Rights Movement Vietnam War Sexual Revolution	Baby Bust Two-earner households with latchkey kids Rise in divorce rates Widespread use of personal computers Raised in era of economic uncertainty (recession, layoffs, etc.) *Challenger* disaster	Grew up with email, Internet, cell phones, and immediate access to information Violence and terrorism in US: Oklahoma City bombing, Columbine High School, Sept. 11 Globalization Most scheduled childhoods in US history
Positive traits ascribed to this generation	Hard-working Idealistic Committed to harmony	Entrepreneurial Flexible and creative Comfortable with technology	Tech-savvy Attuned to and appreciative of diversity Skilled multitaskers
Negative traits ascribed to this generation	Sense of entitlement Workaholics Self-centered	Skeptical and cynical Lazy, slackers Question authority figures	Lacking basic literacy fundamentals Very short attention spans—distracted and distractible Not loyal to employing organization
Workplace attributes	Belief that hard work=long hours Long-term commitment to employing organization	Desire for work-life balance, demand for flexible work schedules Less hierarchical, prefer more flexible structures Expect to have multiple employers, perhaps even multiple careers	Excellent at integrating technology into workplace Demand immediate feedback and recognition Expect to have many employers, multiple careers

Although it is clear based on this research that each generation in the workplace is similar in some aspects and different in others, the question about whether it is something *specific* to the Millennial generation that developed a distinction in their ethical values or if it is merely a matter of their state in life remains. In other words, did their experiences during their formative years bring about their distinctive ethical values or could it be that it was simply a result of being the youngest members of today's workforce? This matter has been among those analyzed by the Ethics Resource Center through comprehensive longitudinal study since 1994. Essentially, their National Business Ethics Survey (NBES) has examined business ethics from an employee's perspective to unveil workplace trends and measure the effectiveness of several programs used by the organizations they studied.

Their research concluded the declared differences in ethical values by Millennials were more likely a result of their work experience and tenure as the most recent entrants into America's workforce, rather than something specifically related to their attributes. Generations were examined as part of the NBES in 2000, 2003, 2005, 2007, 2009 and 2011. NBES consistently found employees who have felt *pressure* to commit misconduct were far more likely to actually observe misconduct than those who do not. Hence, when employees felt *pressure* to compromise their organization's standards of ethical conduct, they were almost always actually observing some wrongdoing as well.

Likewise, for the periods in which the NBES results considered variances by generation, there was no consistent observed trend based on the level of professional experience. For instance, Millennials were not consistently more likely to feel pressure than older workers or vice versa. However, there did tend to be a little variance among rates of pressure for malfeasance when comparing age cohorts.

As illustrated in the chart below, it is evident pressure to engage in misconduct is at an all-time low among all age groups. NBES research also suggests that *pressure* is an age-independent trend – one that is experienced similarly by all generational workers.

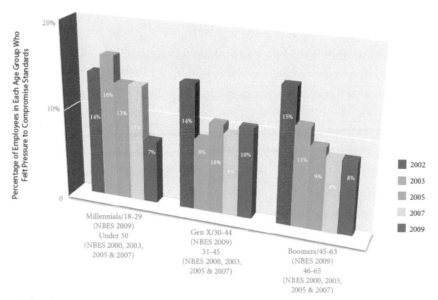

The downward trend of pressure to commit misconduct reversed in 2011, the last year the NBES looked specifically at generations and has remained high ever since. The graphic below expands on the one above graphic by including 2011, and is presented over all the generations. The 2011 level was the highest since 2000, which was before a wave of corporate abuse and scandals triggered a renewed emphasis on corporate ethics.

PRESSURE APPROACHING HIGHEST LEVELS

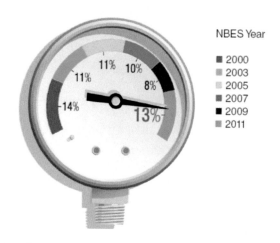

Percentage of employees feeling pressure to compromise standards

The Ethics Resource Center conducted additional Millennial-specific analysis in 2013 versus 2011 NBES, which not only indicated a heightened sensitivity to ethical issues, but also the formation of ethical perspectives not always in the interest of employers. In particular, it noted 49 percent of the observations of workplace unethical behavior were being made by the Millennials (so, the remaining 51 percent covers the observations made by the entirety of older generations), and also that 67 percent of the Millennials who observed such contact also reported it. Unfortunately, this analysis also noted Millennials do not always find certain problematic behaviors, which the indicated percentage of Millennials find to be ethical:

- Using social networking to find out about the company's competitors – 37 percent
- "Friending" a client or customer on a social network – 36 percent
- Uploading personal photos on a company network – 26 percent
- Keeping copies of confidential documents – 22 percent
- Working less to compensate for cuts in benefits or pay – 18 percent
- Buying personal items using a company credit card – 15 percent
- Blogging or tweeting negatively about a company – 14 percent
- Taking a copy of work software home for personal use – 13 percent

Though no longer including the ethical attributes of specific generations, findings in the 2016 NBES imply a deterioration in the practice of business ethics since the 2011 NBES. Overall pressure to commit misconduct reached 22 percent, which is well above the 13 percent level seen in the 2011 NBES. The 2016 NBES found that 33 percent of employees observed unethical behavior, 59 percent of unethical behavior was reported and 36 percent of reporting have experienced a subsequent retaliation. For employees who felt pressure to commit misconduct, 73 percent observed it while of those employees who felt no such pressure, 17 percent observed it. This percentage discrepancy suggests "where there is smoke, there is fire." Another 2016 NBES found that when there was retaliation, it occurred within three weeks 79 percent of the time.

When it comes to ethical values in the workplace, some things transcend age and generational differences, such as an innate desire for fairness and an enthusiasm to work for leaders who are trustworthy and capable. However, age and generations do appear to play a role at times. For instance, when it comes to ethical deeds in the workplace, some groups are more vulnerable, such as

Millennial workers and managers. In particular, the aforementioned 2013 analysis the Ethics Resource Center made of Millennials found that only 56 percent of the Millennials believed "they have influence" at the workplace, as compared to 59 percent of Gen Xers and 84 percent of Boomers. This disconnect likely contributes to the cited improper beliefs that some Millennials hold towards certain ethical situations. Thus, what steps should organizational leaders take to help associates with the challenges they face?

There are ways to ease the burden of the Millennial associates, while protecting the organization and growing its nascent pool of talent. Some examples are as follows:

- Develop an ethics training programs for Millennial workers to enable them to identify and correctly address ethical issues that are common in their industry and positions.
- Develop an ethics training programs for managers that supervise Millennial workers to instruct them how to address and support pressure and retaliation issues that exist.
- Establish mentoring programs that pair Millennials with older, seasoned associates who can lend their experience and nurture them (more details in Chapter Eight).

Although it is clear there are no silver bullets to prevent ethical issues, these suggestions can serve as a starting point to instill a process that can start to mitigate the glaring risks. In addition to the positive influence that these aforementioned programs can have on Millennial workers, organizations should take comfort in the fact that Millennials have been well educated in college regarding the importance of ethics in their workplace. Immediately after numerous scandals in Corporate America during the early 2000s, the Association to Advance Collegiate Schools of Business (AACSB) established an Ethics Education Task Force to detect challenges and opportunities in business ethics education. As the leading U.S. accrediting organization for business degree programs, the AACSB issued a mandate for business ethics education to be a top priority in college programs.

Another contributing factor that has had a positive influence on the Millennials' ethical value system is their upbringing. Based on a survey conducted with 130 juniors and seniors from the Millennial generation, a study by the University of California Santa Barbara in 2009 found that their parents had encouraged altruism (i.e., concern for others) during their youth. As a result, the Center of Information and Research on Civic Learning and Engagement have reported that Millennials are volunteering at historically high rates. However, does this altruistic penchant translate into a strong work ethic for Millennials?

Gallup examined this issue in 2014 and found that the average number of full-time hours per week continues to creep up, as illustrated in the table below. In addition, Gallup found 40 percent of full time workers work more than 50 hours per week, and full-time salaried workers average 49 hours per week, while full-time hourly workers average 44 hours per week. Gallup also found that full time is increasingly encapsulating more than one job, as 50 percent of full-time workers before the Financial Crisis worked exclusively at one job, which has now dipped to 43 percent. Earlier research, conducted by the Family and Work Institute, found no differences between the hours worked by Millennials during their 20s than Gen Xers or Boomers during this stage of their career. Thus, they concluded that work ethic (as measured by time) was identical.

The growing number of work hours notwithstanding, there has been a growing trend to decrease centrality of work within people's lives, particularly among Millennials. As the following chart (from a ManpowerGroup study) indicates, a mere 13 percent of Millennials aspire to leadership as a top career priority.

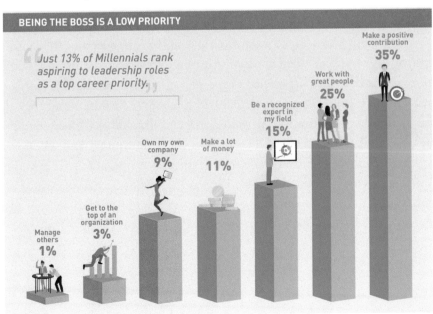

For organizational leaders, this will complicate their succession planning efforts because there will be fewer applicants to choose among in comparison to the past. For Millennials, this should create a greater opportunity for those that have leadership aspirations with their employing organization.

In 2010, Pew Research found that only Millennials did not have "work ethic" in their self-ascribed "top five identifying features." Meanwhile, Boomers listed work ethic at the top of their list, Gen Xers had it second and the Silent generation had it fourth. While now somewhat dated research, this Millennial reputation seems to still hold. Although this certainly does not imply that work ethic is not important to Millennials, it does indicate that it is not something they identify themselves by. Hence, this could be a precursor for the shift from a traditional work ethic.

In fact, the individuality Millennials strive for sometimes translates to very hard work. A 2016 "Project: Time Off" study found a greater propensity of "work martyrs" among Millennials (43 percent) than earlier generations (29 percent). Work Martyr "symptoms" are identified by the following statements: 1) "No one else at my company can do the work while I'm away;" 2) "I want to show complete dedication to my company and my job;" 3) "I don't want others to think I am replaceable;" and 4) "I feel guilty for using my paid time off." The study also found 52 percent of Millennials said it was acceptable to answer a work e-mail during dinner, versus 22 percent of Boomers.

Work ethic is developed from the upbringing, lifestyle, and the cultural pulse of a generation. Where the senior generations were raised to work within the confines that the corporations have set and adjust to meet the needs of their organization, Millennials were raised to speak their mind, challenge the boundaries that organizations have defined, and demand that their employer adjust to meet their needs. This clash between traditional and Millennial work philosophies is challenging the basic unspoken rules that have governed organizations for decades. As shown in this chart, Millennials are resisting the status quo.

Traditional Work Ethic	Millennial Work Ethic
Work comes first	Life comes first
Distinctions between work and personal time	No distinction between work and personal time (work/life integration)
Follow the rules no matter what.	Follow the rules that work and make their own rules if they do not.
The boss deserves respect	Equality and respect should only be given when it has been earned
9 to 5 with overtime expected	No defined work clock
Preference for face-to-face contact	Preference for digital contact
Dress the part at all times	Dress the part when necessary
Will change to meet the needs of the organization	Expect the organization to change to meet their needs

For organizational leaders, the real question is: how can you "successfully" integrate your Millennial associates into your workplace given these philosophical differences? For the Millennials, the blunt question is: how can we get an organization to empathize with us?

One strategy that has proven to be very successful for both organizational leaders and Millennials at various Fortune 500 organizations is Leadership Development classes. In this program, organizational leaders would combine their traditional courses on vision, values, integrity, communication, influence, emotional intelligence and image with newly designed business decorum training. In order for these programs to be effective, it is vital that they are interactive with leadership-caliber associates from the Millennial generation. This course will not only be highly valued by this generation that "thrives" on continued education and mentoring opportunities, but will help them engage with your organization.

For instance, a leadership development course on *How to be Influential* could also address the issue of chain of command from both the organizational and associate's point of view. Another example is an Effective Communication class that would also address a decorum expectation when working with senior management or business customers. The reason these types of programs have worked successfully (when executed properly) is the setting in which they take place. In other words, when the training environment is non-demeaning and interactive (meaning both the organizational leaders and Millennials have the opportunity to express their stance in a collegial atmosphere), it makes it much easier for learning to take place and empower both parties to seek first to understand each other. The desire to learn and grow is a distinguishing trait that separates Millennials from the prior generations in the workforce. Learning management systems (LMS), certification programs and workplace training opportunities are not just attractive perks, but necessary toward engaging and retaining these employees.

To that end, while generational differences are not myths, making decisions based on a stereotype is just as harmful as ignoring the differences altogether. Hence, engaging principal stakeholders of all generations in conversations will lead to improved decisions, stronger organizations and a better understanding of how leadership between generations can bridge this growing cultural gap. Moreover, it is imperative to seek *mutual* solutions. To that end, what are some other practical recommendations that can align ethical values?

As discussed, Millennials must fight through the allure of turning a blind eye to ethical violations in order to protect the integrity of their organization. It will continue to be a challenge given the peril of retaliation. However, Millennials should remember they are tacitly endorsing the misconduct if they choose not to report it. Additionally, it is vital that after they report ethical violations through proper channels, they keep it confidential and not discuss it with friends or blog about it. According to the previous referenced 2013 Ethics Resource Center report, Millennials thought associated posting on their personal social network pages was acceptable: 40 percent regarding feelings about one's job, 26 percent regarding progress on a work project, 19 percent regarding information about a company competitors and 16 percent regarding an opinion about a co-workers politics.

This same research by the Ethics Resource Center revealed that nearly one out of five Millennials feels it is *acceptable* to make copies of confidential documents at work. It is vital that Millennials understand this not only violates their company's ethics policy, but may lead organizations to question if they are capable of protecting proprietary data.

For organizational leaders, it is imperative that they adopt the virtue of "spiritual meekness." For clarity, this is not the Merriam-Webster Dictionary word that is defined as mild, deficient in courage, submissive or weak. It is the spiritual definition that means a total "lack" of self-pride in Greek (i.e. prautes). This leadership virtue toward followers demonstrates a benevolent compassion for subordinates. However, this ethical virtue is not about giving up power, but rather diligently harnessing it for the good of associates.

Thus, if organizational leaders make a conscious decision to act *spiritually meek* (since it is not innate), this selfless virtue will not only swiftly gain associates' trust when it is sincere, but will start to align the leaders' ethical values to the organization's benefit.

Chapter Eight

Developing Collaborative Relationships

"Members of this generation want a clear career path laid out for them. They already know where they are going. And they expect you to make sure they get there"

This quote from *Human Resource Executive* magazine personifies the Millennial generation's desire for its leaders to collaborate with them to achieve their career goals. However, this clearly is easier said than done. Given the challenges expressed in the prior chapters, how can organizational leaders and Millennials effectively collaborate with one another to tender a mutual benefit? This question was studied in depth in the survey given to Millennials referenced in the Introduction. Ultimately, these findings revealed insights which at times conflicted with preconceived notions about their preferences.

For instance, a survey conducted by Robert Half International and Yahoo! HotJobs indicated that "Pay and Benefits" were considered the most important factor for Millennials in their career decisions. In fact, one-third of the Millennial respondents identified such in this survey. Conversely, when Millennials were asked the same question in the survey referenced in the Introduction, "Pay and Benefits" ranked fifth at 9 percent, behind work-life balance (34 percent), career progression (30 percent), challenging assignment (15 percent), and work environment (12 percent). More recently, the "Staples Advantage Workplace Index" survey in 2015 found that the overall priority of salary for Millennials had now climbed to 29 percent but with much of the remaining priority connected to "non-traditional benefits," the five cited examples being 1) Flexibility in where they work; 2) Office perks presenting a positive culture; 3) Improved breakrooms and improved break time; 4) Concern for the environment; and 5) Trust in leadership and a relationship with their direct boss. Given this dynamic, what explains such changes in the survey results?

The simple answer is *experience*. The first survey was conducted approximately five years before the one cited in the Introduction. Thus, this research (along with other studies on this topic) has clearly indicated that the longer a Millennial is employed in the workforce, the greater chance their priorities may alter based on their circumstances. Not surprisingly, this phenomenon has been observed in all prior generations in the workforce as well. Hence, these surveys must be given regularly to sustain a pulse on their priorities.

Based on the Millennial feedback in these surveys and numerous research that has explored effective techniques to create a collaborative environment in the workplace, it is clear there is no magic bullet. However, three strategies that have proven to be beneficial, particularly for the Millennials are: provide feedback on a frequent basis, assign a mentor to them (to acclimate them into the organization), and create a teamwork-oriented culture. Ultimately, this strategy will not only enrich Millennials, but their organizations as well.

A 2015 *Harvard Business Review* article observed the much higher priority that Millennials put on managerial feedback, as opposed to older generations. The significant difference is seen in the following chart. A 2015 *Forbes* article posits that the reasons for Millennials preferring such frequent feedback are 1) needing assurance that management is approachable; 2) it is what they are used to; 3) preferring to tackle issues early in and make small adjustments; 4) wanting to engage with talented and professional people; and 5) wanting to be able to apply feedback immediately.

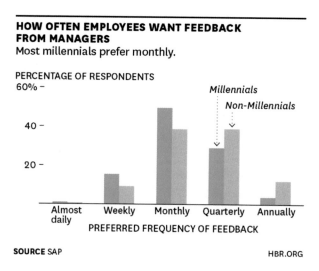

HOW OFTEN EMPLOYEES WANT FEEDBACK FROM MANAGERS
Most millennials prefer monthly.

PERCENTAGE OF RESPONDENTS

Millennials
Non-Millennials

Almost daily | Weekly | Monthly | Quarterly | Annually
PREFERRED FREQUENCY OF FEEDBACK

SOURCE SAP   HBR.ORG

The challenge is the vast majority of American companies are currently providing associate performance reviews on an annual basis, a practice which is in conflict with the Millennial expectations. Thus, it would behoove organizational leaders to re-evaluate the standard procedures and potentially increase the frequency to quarterly in order to meet their Millennial associates' fervent desire for continuous feedback from their manager. Further, given this primary change, should the feedback continue to be as formal?

Based on the responses received from Millennials in this book's research survey, the answer was an emphatic "no." As a matter of fact, research from numerous academic studies indicated that Millennials would *prefer* that feedback be more informal in order to reduce stress that accompanies it. Thus, should organizations consider a change in mode?

Millennial respondents from the aforementioned survey indicated their preferred communication method for their performance reviews and feedback sessions (with their manager) was face-to-face by a notable majority (76 percent). Conversely, asynchronous communication (i.e., e-mail or online) was preferred by less than 9 percent. This may astonish some pundits that believe a Millennials' digital propensity will prevail in these scenarios. Thus, these compelling insights should serve as a wake-up call to organizations to either adapt to quarterly performance reviews (delivering them face-to-face) for their Millennial associates or implement more frequent, informal feedback sessions for them throughout the year. Either way, it is clear Millennials want to hear from their managers more frequently than the customary practice in a more informal and synchronous setting. This paradigm shift will not only engage and motivate Millennials more effectively, but has proven to notably increase the odds of retaining them (more on this in Chapter Nine).

The next issue to address in an effort to develop more collaborative relationships is *how* to communicate most effectively with Millennials during reviews and feedback sessions. When communicating with Millennials, it is vital to be *positive* in the manner in which the message is conveyed, clear with expectations and concise in its delivery. First, the message crafted by the organizational leader should utilize positive reinforcement and be constructive in nature. Recall that this generation was raised by parents who positively affirmed their choices. Consequently, the workplace is frequently the first time they have received negative feedback so it is essential to keep this in mind when coaching them on opportunities for development. Second, it is vital to be clear about expectations to avoid ambiguity. Since they were raised as a "scripted" generation with firm instructions, they expect clarity. Finally, their instant-gratification mindset desires a concise message. More generally, as a result of the close supervision Millennials have had at every moment of their lives, they may require specific instructions on everything from appropriate attire to how to prepare a memo in their workplace. This is because this "scripted" generation grew up with parents that were more protective and provided more hands-on support for many aspects of their life. While this may be a real challenge for the independent manager who prefers to work autonomously, it could make supervision easier as they can give instructions once to a group and benefit from team results. Thus, although there may be some challenges ahead, Millennials are a dynamic group who bring a unique ability to adapt and collaborate. In addition, it is important for organizational leaders not to lament with Millennials about the olden days when people had *respect*. Rather, just describe the behavior that is expected of them, why it is expected, and then move on. This lamenting behavior merely dwells on history that has evolved, rather than focusing on their future.

Another example of a common issue among a multi-generational workforce that may need to be addressed is the use of technological devices (particularly smartphones) during meetings. Because Millennials are "always connected" to the Internet, these devices are simply another means for them to access information. Hence, if corporate policy prohibits use of these devices during meetings, it is important that organizational leaders bring this policy to the attention of their staff, particularly Millennials who may not be aware of this decorum. In the event that it just becomes too challenging to request associates to cease accessing their phones, an effective method that has been used by numerous large corporations is to put a "cell phone box" in the center of the meeting table and require that all attendees place their phone in it (unless they have a legitimate emergency-level need that requires it to be accessible).

In the event that the organizational leader can not effectively manage this policy, it is recommended to have a human resources manager provide a training session on this topic, which could also cover other policies, such as appropriate dress or exposed tattoos.

The second strategy that has proven to be beneficial for the Millennials generation in the workplace is *mentoring*. Unlike their Gen X counterparts, who treat their managers as colleagues, Millennials prefer and thrive on mentoring relationships with their leaders. Essentially, the mentoring relationship feeds the Millennials' avid desire for positive and continuous feedback from their leadership. In addition, it provides an environment in the workplace that is conducive to frequent collaboration with peers and affirmation from their manager. Given this fundamental shift from Gen X, what factors drove this change?

At the outset, it is important to remember that Millennials were raised in a closely supervised and often overprotective environments. Moreover, they have received specific instructions for almost everything they do from parents who have treated them as friends. Ultimately, Millennials expect special attention because they were raised being told how special they were in school, on television, and in the home. Now it is management's turn. Given this *hands-on* upbringing, it should be of no surprise that Millennials actively seek out mentors in the workforce for this support, communication, and personalized attention.

Additionally, Millennials have proven to be very values-driven, with the need to see the connection between their personal aspirations, core values and the organization's vision and goals. Likewise, they aspire to understand the "big picture" and feel a part of something special, and not just a "cog in the wheel." Hence, organizational leaders need to create opportunities to engage them in meaningful working relationships that provide on-going training, opportunities that challenge them and meaningful work that stretches their capabilities. Consequently, advancement and recognition is often more important to them than financial compensation. To that end, no method has proven to meet these needs and fulfill these desires more than mentoring. Thus, what exactly does mentoring entail?

Mentoring is a partnership between a leader and follower. It essentially involves a leader coaching and infusing their skills into a follower. It is follower-focused, meaning it concentrates on developing the skills of the protégé, rather than on the mentor. Thus, it is more evident in leaders that put their people before themselves, which are also known as servant leaders. When a leader takes this approach and makes it apparent they are putting the follower's interests first, it will often convict a follower to collegially surrender to the mentoring process. When executed properly, mentoring can fast track these relationships.

The key for a mentoring relationship to work is *trust*. When Millennials sincerely believe that their mentor has their best interest at heart, this relationship can transcend a trust that is paramount for this relationship to authentically exist. Conversely, when it is evident (or perceived) by Millennials that their mentor has not put their interest first, the rapport may never build the trust necessary for the relationship to flourish. As Zig Ziglar said, "People truly don't care how much you know until they know how much you care."

When structuring mentorship programs for Millennials, it is important to consider an individual's style, openness to the relationship and desire for success. In other words, the mentor and Millennial protégé must have compatible styles with both interested in the relationship with the selfless goals and with the organization's benefit at heart. However, there is no evidence that their age difference needs to be at any specific spread.

In the end, the benefits of a mentoring program may go both ways. Benefits to the Millennial protégé may be more apparent when it comes to learning their organization's policies and decorum. Conversely, the benefits to the mentor are normally received in the way of returning to their fundamentals to revisit best practices that made them successful. They can also benefit from their protégé by learning generational skills (i.e. technology).

The third strategy that has shown to be beneficial for Millennials in the workplace is a *teamwork-oriented* culture. Since their youngest days, Millennials have been on some type of "team" or involved in an organized activity. As a result, Millennial associates will expect to be a part of, and excel in, group projects in the workplace. Moreover, they view group-based work to be more fun and are more comfortable in this environment based on their upbringing. Likewise, empirical evidence suggests that Millennials value teamwork and are accustomed to team collaboration more than prior generations. Hence, Millennial workers are more likely to be actively involved, fully committed and contribute their best efforts to their organization when their work tasks are performed in a collaborative team.

However, it should be noted that some research has noted downside to teams. For instance, some organizations have found that Millennial workers find excessive comfort in team-based direction, oversight and decision making. Their primary concern was that Millennials appeared to avoid risk associated with independent thinking and decisions by working in a team-setting too often. This legitimate concern has merit in several studies. Another concern was that a teamwork-oriented culture took longer to make decisions by consensus. Thus, when decisions need to occur quickly, teamwork hindered the process.

Another negative implication of self-managed teamwork is the concertive control that naturally emerges from this environment. Research has shown that the control within teams is negotiated and manifested through formal and informal team-based interactions, causing its participants to develop a shared sense of responsibility for the team's success. While this may sound harmless, the real issue comes when members feel that they must gain compliance from the group causing associates to conform to mutually agreed norms. Consider the consequences if this group is comprised of heterogeneous members.

On the other hand, Pew Research suggests that Millennials are less prone to, and even verbally resistant to, these communicative forms of control in their workgroups due to their self-assured and individualistic nature. Hence, it would behoove organizational leaders to observe this dynamic personally within their respective companies before they indict Millennials with these charges. Regardless whether there is any substitutive proof, it is clear that Millennials have a strong desire to work in teams and will likely request it.

In summary, developing collaborative relationships in the workplace involves a *mutual* respect that must go both ways. For Millennials, this means conveying gratitude for leaders who are willing to serve as a mentor, expressing appreciation for managers if they offer additional feedback opportunities and accepting responsibilities that involve group and individual assignments for the organization. For organizational leaders, this means treating Millennial associates as valued team members even if when it should be obvious. Remember the Golden Rule: "Do unto others as you would have them do unto you." Ultimately, this timeless and eternal proverb will never fail.

Chapter Nine

Cultivating Loyalty in the Workplace

"Seventy percent of Millennials say there is a strong possibility they will change jobs once the economy improves."

This quote from SBR Consulting likely causes great anxiety for organizations that employ Millennials. Given their history of "job hopping" on average six to seven times in their 20s, it should be of no surprise why this new generation has earned the reputation of a *disloyal* workforce. When organizational leaders calculate the additional cost they incur to replace a Millennial associate from the training investment to the lost production while a new employee is hired, it translates into both a human resources and financial matter for them to lament over. Moreover, there may also be an impact to the current workforce that the organization needs to address from the speculation that spreads when someone leaves.

This bears the real question: What is "loyalty" and how should it be defined? For organizations, *loyalty* from Millennial associates means an allegiance to them with a bias for action and passion to see their organization succeed. For Millennial associates, *loyalty* means their organization will present them with enough opportunities for growth. Hence, loyalty exists based on the perspective from which it is viewed. To that end, this chapter will seek to cultivate loyalty from *both* of these perspectives so that Millennial associates and their respective organizations can realize this highly desired virtue. In an ultra competitive market, this virtue is often the final determinant for the top Millennials.

In theory, the Millennial generation view their commitment to being loyal to their organization as genuine. Recall that the Qualtrics study cited earlier found that 89 percent of Millennials "expected to stay with their current employer for 10 or more years," but this was based on the underlying expectation that there would be regular compensation increases and opportunities for advancement. Millennials regard loyalty to be a contract that is frequently invalidated by their employer when the organization does not satisfy the Millennial's expectations. In a 2015 report, Gallup termed Millennials the "Job Hopping Generation," finding that 60 percent of them, as compared to 45 percent of Non-Millennials, are "open to a new opportunity," and that 36 percent of them will "look for a new job in a different organization once the current job market improves," versus the 21 percent of Non-Millennials who say the same. This same Gallup report noted that job turnover by Millennials costs the U.S. economy some $30.5 billion annually.

Hence, it is imperative for organizational leaders to attain an astute understanding of the Millennials' *expectations* in order to reverse this trend and start to cultivate loyalty in their workplace. This matter was examined in depth in the survey given to Millennials that was referenced in the introduction of this book. Ultimately, this research concluded that Millennials could be loyal under certain conditions. Case in point, more than half of the Millennials surveyed said they expect to stay with their current employer for at least five years, and 28 percent indicated they will likely remain with their organization for a decade or more *if* their expectations were met. The primary contributing factor was their opportunities for career advancement. The secondary contributing factors were pay and benefits, further education and work-life balance. In addition, 88 percent of respondents said they felt a sense of loyalty to their organization if they are promoted regularly and compensated fairly. Although what constitutes *regularly* and *fairly* is up for debate, these responses demonstrate that Millennials are not seeking change just for the sake of change.

While this survey provided a deeper understanding about why Millennials remain with their prevailing organizations, it did not answer the question: "Why do they leave?" A 2016 *Forbes* article suggests that a near term departure may be inevitable unless the Millennials' employer has adequately communicated what the company stands for and what makes it different, provided growth opportunities in the last year, and promotes more sufficient managerial approachability that concerns about lacking meaningful responsibilities can be promptly addressed. According to Peter Sheahan, a renowned expert on the Millennial generation, "If there is an absence of a clear career path, a Millennial employee's only option is out." In other words, Sheahan argues that Millennials will inevitably leave their employer if they do not clearly understand the career path available to them, and the time it should take to achieve goals. Millennial surveys conducted by Pew Research concluded likewise in their analogous work studies. For organizational leaders, this evidence should serve as a wake-up call to provide a clear career path for their Millennial associates, or risk losing them.

Another factor contributing to the generational change in organizational loyalty is the Millennials' cultural lens that developed during their rearing. For instance, Millennial children watched their loyal parents get laid off as the economy shifted in the 1990s. The resulting message was that organization loyalty was a value developed by people, but not always honored by corporations. The Millennials observed a disconnect that continues to play out in the on-going shift from the once unwavering loyalty championed by the Silent generation to the skepticism expressed by Millennials today. However, it should be noted that when trust exists in spite of this, Millennials have shown firm loyalty to their boss.

An *Accounting Web* article (2017), "Four Ways to Attract and Engage Millennials at Your Firm," suggests Millennials would find the following attractive: 1) the ability to call some of their own shots (workplace flexibility); 2) an employer that lends a helping hand (to their community); 3) someone who invests in them (professional development); and 4) employers who "stay on their toes" (make workplace rules changes as needed).

Another dynamic that should be taken into consideration when evaluating *loyalty* in the Millennial generation is the amount of student loans they have accumulated while pursuing higher education. In 2017, Experian reported the average outstanding student loan debt was approximately $34,000, and that total student debt had risen from $800 billion in 2007 to $1.4 trillion in 2017. Consequently, Millennial associates will often jump jobs in order to help pay off their student loan debt, according to Carolyn Ockels, managing partner at Emergent Research. Conversely, if an organization is willing to pay off their Millennial associates' student loans in lieu of a bonus program, this could carry a positive effect and potentially retain the employee for at least the required vesting period.

Given these challenges, the question is, "What else can organizations do to retain Millennial associates, particularly the high performers?" Firstly, their compensation must be commensurate with their industry or they can be recruited away fairly easily according to research conducted by Robert

Half International and the Pew Research Center. In fact, both of these studies suggested offering a compensation package that is slightly *above* the prevailing industry rate reported by the Department of Labor's Bureau of Labor Statistics on an annual basis. Moreover, they recommend making an up-front offer that is attractive out of the gate, rather than proposing a lower starting salary that offers the possibility of a raise or bonus in six months. This will appeal to the Millennial's desire for instant results.

Another equally important issue that is diligently considered by Millennials when selecting an employer is the overall benefit package. Studies have shown that Millennials have serious concerns about the rising cost of healthcare and solvency of the U.S. Social Security system. Thus, Millennials want the very best healthcare and retirement benefits available, so it is crucial for organizations to emphasize their perks when recruiting them. A Fidelity Investments study (2018) found that 57 percent of Millennials are seeking a better spend-now/save-for-the-future balance, and that current millennial spending priorities are essential living expenses (38 percent), building an emergency fund (34 percent) and saving more for retirement (33 percent). And Bank of America and Wells Fargo respectively supplied the below recent data which illustrate the long-term financial security concerns and current personal financial management priorities of Millennials.

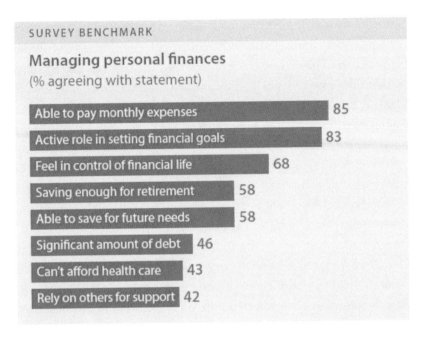

SURVEY BENCHMARK

Managing personal finances
(% agreeing with statement)

Able to pay monthly expenses	85
Active role in setting financial goals	83
Feel in control of financial life	68
Saving enough for retirement	58
Able to save for future needs	58
Significant amount of debt	46
Can't afford health care	43
Rely on others for support	42

Once the compensation and benefit package table stakes are met, Millennials will focus on the items that cultivate loyalty to their employing organization. The question "what's more important in your *first* job," asked in the Allstate Heartland Monitor Poll (2015), revealed somewhat different responses for "old people" (defined as those over age 30 and those 25 to 29 with career experience) and "young people" (defined as those age 18 to 24 and those 25 to 29 lacking career experience). The responses of "old people" were Money (33 percent), Learning Skills (31 percent), Enjoyment (16 percent) and Making a Difference (11 percent). Meanwhile, the responses of "young people" were Money (16 percent), Learning Skills (23 percent), Enjoyment (32 percent) and Making a Difference (25 percent). Thus, employers should choose specific recruiting pitches by age and experience. With a 50/50 weighting to each group, the overall response to "what's most important in a *first* job" priorities could be: Learning New Skills (27 percent), Money (25 percent), Enjoyment (24 percent) and Making a Difference (18 percent).

In order for organizations to truly understand their Millennial associates' career concerns, they should consider these issues from their viewpoint. To that end, what are the Millennials seeking in a boss, in their work environment and in their career path?

As previously stated, the Millennials desire an approachable and trustworthy boss who provides regular feedback. Of these attributes, the most important for them is trust. This may have resulted from their skepticism in the stock market that subjugated them when they began investing (the "Lost Decade" of 2000-2009). In addition, Millennials have developed a lack of trust for financial institutions ever since the Great Recession. Thus, it is key for organizational leaders to build credibility (and establish trust) with Millennial by following through on commitments and modeling proper behavior to avoid hypocrisy. Fortunately for organizational leaders, Millennial skepticism has not carried over to the boss without cause. In other words, Millennials appear to have given their bosses the benefit of the doubt and not indicted them based on a widespread cynicism.

The "2018 Deloitte Millennial Survey" suggests that the prospects for this "benefit of the doubt" continuing indefinitely may now be at risk. There has been a considerable reversal in a favorable trend in Millennial views of corporate motives:

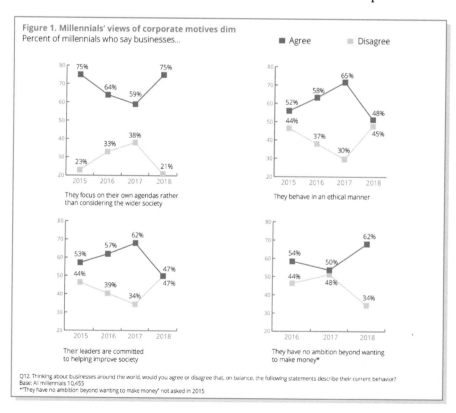

Figure 1. Millennials' views of corporate motives dim
Percent of millennials who say businesses...

■ Agree   ■ Disagree

They focus on their own agendas rather than considering the wider society

They behave in an ethical manner

Their leaders are committed to helping improve society

They have no ambition beyond wanting to make money*

Q12. Thinking about businesses around the world, would you agree or disagree that, on balance, the following statements describe their current behavior?
Base: All millennials 10,455
*"They have no ambition beyond wanting to make money" not asked in 2015

Fortunately, this same survey does not indicate Millennials have lost hope in the ability of businesses to positively contribute to needed societal changes. "As in last year's report, three quarters of young workers see multinational corporations as having the potential to help solve society's economic, environmental and social challenges," states the accompanying report. "Respondents feel that business could be particularly effective in the areas of education, skills and training, economic stability, and cybersecurity."

Once trust is established, it is important for organizational leaders to initiate open dialogue with their Millennial associates to encourage interaction and make it evident that their contribution is welcomed. Case in point, Millennials often feel that if their boss does not tell them they are doing a good job, they will assume that their work is deficient. This penchant is counter to the "no news is good news" outlook of Gen X and Baby Boomers who assume if they do not hear from their boss, their work is satisfactory. In addition, it is important to provide feedback that is clear and frequent in order to meet Millennial associates' expectations in the workplace. This step is critical to Millennial retention.

Millennials regard frequent feedback as a way of measuring whether they are on track to succeed in their job. To that end, a Qualtrics survey (2017) examined the "top five things Millennials want when they start a new job." It found the considerations to be 1) "I am sufficiently trained" (40 percent); 2) "My expectations and goals are clearly defined" (31 percent); 3) "I am provided all the information needed to do my job" (30 percent); 4) "I am given reasonable goals and timelines" (26 percent); and 5) "My leaders seem to be invested in my success" (23 percent). However, this survey also determined that desiring frequent feedback should not be equated with satisfaction regarding lacking autonomy, as "my boss spends time to help me" was supported by only 15 percent. And unlike the previous generations, Millennials expect frequent contact with *their* leadership in order to have *their* voice heard and *their* input considered in organizational decisions. This issue is essential for Millennial engagement in the workplace.

The second factor Millennials have cited as "critically important" in their decision process when evaluating whether they should remain with their prevailing organization is the work environment. Thus, environment plays a pivotal role in influencing Millennials loyalty to an organization. When Millennials were asked to describe some characteristics of the "ideal" work environment (for the survey referenced in the Introduction), their general responses to this open-ended question (in order of priority) were as follows:

- Friendly, supportive, no drama and non-threatening (mentioned most often)
- Team-orientation that is conducive to sharing their insights with other peers
- Open communication, approachable management team, no bureaucracy
- Challenging, stimulating and engaging work setting (avoiding the mundane)
- Seeking the opportunity to contribute and be heard (i.e., work is valued)
- Relaxed, casual and laid-back atmosphere; professional attire is not required

The chart below compares the observed responses (including depiction of frequency).

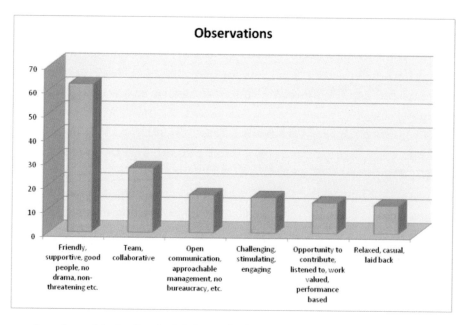

Based on this feedback, Millennials demonstrate a strong proclivity for a collegial environment that is free of drama and conflict in the workplace. In addition, they prefer a team-oriented environment that feeds collaborative interaction and a casual atmosphere that is conducive to making friends in the workplace. What may surprise some is the type of interaction they prefer. While this digital generation is always connected to the Internet and the dominant participant in social networking, two-thirds of Millennials revealed that they would prefer to communicate with their coworkers *in-person*, according to a survey by Robert Half International and Yahoo!. Only one in five prefers e-mail communication.

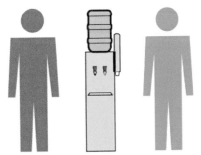

'Let's Meet at the Water Cooler'

Surprise! Two-thirds of the "wired generation" favor in-person conversations with coworkers over other types of communication

The third aspect that Millennials have indicated plays a major role in their loyalty to their employing organization is a well structured, defined and challenging career path. This multi-tasking generation has a mantra of "what's happening next" in the workforce. In the aforementioned Strauss and Howe survey of 800 Millennial college graduates in the workforce, 72 percent fervently expressed a desire for a well-structured career path. As a result of a highly structured upbringing by their Boomer parents, Millennials have grown to dislike ambiguity. In addition, they were told they "can do anything they set their mind to," so having to go through a "probationary period" is foreign to them.

To that end, Millennials associates want to feel like part of a team from day one. Millennials perform at a higher level when they understand how they fit in organizational goals. Thus, do not hold them back from participating in a project simply because they haven't completed training or orientation. This will confuse Millennials and eventually frustrate them in the workplace. Assigning them to a capable manager is also important, as Millennials will become frustrated when put in a position where they answer to a superior lacking foresight into how to effectively plan and execute a project. Moreover, they expect challenging and meaningful assignments. Millennials are committed to furthering their careers and do not want to wait more than three years for a promotion. If they do not feel fulfilled and professionally inspired in their role, they are more likely to be on the lookout for positions elsewhere that will. Hence, remember that boredom is the kiss of death to Millennials. Consequently, it is in a leader's best interest to offer Millennials meaningful responsibilities, difficult tasks and ample opportunities for professional development to propel a stronger sense of loyalty to their organization.

Ultimately, a well-defined and challenging career path can clearly indicate to a Millennial associate what they need to do to succeed in the workplace. However, this is easier said than done. Thus, use the following strategies with Millennial workers:

- **Ideal Skill Set** – Detail what skills, experience and level of education they need to succeed in each position they are interested. This approach will focus them on the skills that are necessary to build, rather than resisting *paying their dues.*
- **Timeline for Promotions** – Set realistic expectations by establishing a timeline for promotions. This prescriptive plan commits a timeframe to Millennials that will feed their need to know what to expect rather than lament over uncertainty.
- **Career Progression** – Work with Millennial associates toward a specific career direction or position. Because they are goal-oriented, Millennials will flourish and work harder in an entry-level position if they know that it is a stepping stone.

Accordingly, these strategies will not only quench the Millennial associates' thirst for a defined and challenging career path, but will accelerate their career development as well. In summary, the recipe for cultivating *loyalty* in the workplace is to establish clear expectations for Millennial associates and organizational leaders alike. Furthermore, it is vital to revisit expectations regularly and compromise when possible. For Millennials, this means taking time to understand that their desire for hands-on management is distinct from prior generations so it may take their boss a little time to get acclimated to this new style. For organizational leaders, this means considering changes in the work environment that demonstrate flexibility yet is not disruptive to the business, such as offering Wi-Fi access to associates (particularly Millennials) during lunch for their mobile devices. In the end, such a compromise could also attract new Millennial recruits into your "Starbucks-like" café.

Chapter Ten

Motivating the Millennial Workforce

"Motivation is a fire from within. If someone else tries to light that fire under you, chances are it will burn very briefly."

This quote from Stephen R. Covey, author of *7 Habits of Highly Effective People*, expresses the importance of internal motivation versus external motivation. Although we all need a little ego rubbing to keep us going from time to time (i.e. external motivation), it is *internal motivation* that really increases our associates' ability to be more successful in the workplace via superior productivity, greater autonomy, and improved self-reliance from their intrinsic desire to do well (as opposed to relying on external factors to spur it).

Unfortunately, there is a "motivational" shift occurring in the social landscape of today's new generation of workers that is exacerbating this matter. More specifically, the Millennials have shown a penchant to be more dependent on external motivation, such as praise and recognition, in the workplace relative to past generations. Case in point, more than a third of Millennial associates surveyed in a recent *Harvard Business Review* study identified as high-potential by their organization admitted they did not put all their effort into their job unless external motivation was offered. In other words, internal motivation was not enough to drive them. Conversely, the other generations in this survey indicated much more reliance on internal motivation and placed considerably less emphasis on external motivators. To that end begs the question, "What caused this motivational shift?"

By and large, Millennials were raised by their parents with the idea that no matter what they do, they are important and should receive recognition and/or reward regardless of their behavior or performance. Thus, one of the consequences of this upbringing is an expectation to be recognized and rewarded for everything – even when results are paltry.

As previously noted, Millennials were raised with a healthy dose of accolades and praise at home, at school and within their communities where recognition and a sense of excelling, often without work or reason, were the focus, rather than constructive criticism and learning how to lose. Ultimately, never "losing" means never learning from mistakes, and therefore, tended to limit development of an internal drive based on a need and desire to improve. Hence, without failing periodically, how can one learn to do better or learn where one excels? These lessons (or lack thereof) only grow stronger the older we get if left uncorrected. Moreover, many Baby Boomer parents advocated for the self-inflation movement, which encouraged Millennials to inflate their self-evaluations.

The result of these influences is a generation (Millennials) that, while believing itself to be internally motivated and driven to succeed, is in fact extrinsically motivated. Thus, Millennials reflect this lack of self-awareness when it comes to motivational needs. The disservice of constant kudos and praise (regardless of accomplishment) has created a false sense of internal motivation and a need for recurring external motivation. However, the catch-22 is that without personal attention, constant praise and creative strategies to satisfy Millennials' external motivation, their productivity and commitment will suffer. In light of this challenge, the question is, "How can organizational leaders coach Millennials to be driven more by internal motivation?" Moreover, "Is it their ultimate responsibility?"

Based on numerous field studies, one of the most responsive methods to invoke a Millennials internal drive (i.e. intrinsic motivation) is to provide them the *why* before the *what* when coaching them. In other words, before organizational leaders describe what a project entails, they should take the time to explain the purpose of it (the why) in order to help them see the "big picture" and hopefully get their commitment to want to contribute.

It is apparent based on empirical studies conducted with the Millennial generation that they care deeply about a lot of things, particularly philanthropic causes. For example, philanthropy is well-regarded in Seattle. The executive director of a non-profit that brings corporations and people together to volunteer in the community, was quoted in a 2017 *MediaMark* article as saying, "Employee volunteerism is an HR issue. Smart companies realize this." In the same article, a Zillow executive was quoted as saying "Millennials need to feel their own agency. They need to feel like they are part of changing the world, in whatever small way that they are, and so we at Zillow recognize that and provide various opportunities for Millennials to do that." Ultimately, intrinsic motivation in the workplace should be defined as the ability to "find meaning in our daily work and to see how their contribution matters." The following two infographics from the aforementioned ManPower Group study detail aspects of Millennials ambitions and perceptions.

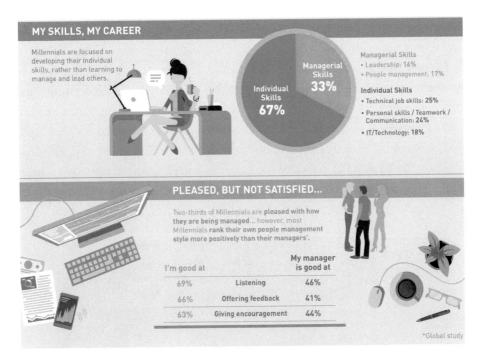

When this is achieved, it will not only serve as a template for success with the Millennials, but has also shown to have the same impact on the other generations in the workforce. Therefore, the leader's role should be to inspire their associates to find the purpose in their work so there is meaning behind their efforts. Additionally, numerous research studies have shown remarkable benefits for Millennial associates when given an opportunity to see their impact on a project in which they were helped bring to fruition.

Although organizational leaders should be admired if they are able to inspire their associates internally, the reality is that most Millennials are motivated by external forces. Thus, "where" and "how" should the Millennial generation be engaged in the workplace?

Any organizational leader who has been put in charge of a corporate motivational or incentive program knows that half the battle is getting the associates to use it over the long term. After the initial set-up, most programs will die on the vine because they either are not meaningful or do not reside in the same place as the associates for whom they are targeted. Thus, the old adage is "fish where they fish" and anyone who knows Millennials know these fish swim on Facebook and Instagram. In fact, a PriceWaterhouseCoppers survey found that 96 percent of Millennials in the U.S. workforce belong to an online social network, with Facebook continuing to lead the pack.

Hence, for organizations that are open to allowing Facebook, this may just be the perfect home for your next incentive program to externally motivate them. As opposed to old-fashioned reward programs that may never be reviewed by Millennials, Facebook is easily accessible where they "virtually" live and can be updated in real-time. In addition, this venue allows the organization to recognize Millennial associate among their friends. Bear in mind that most Millennials, and some Gen X associates, use Facebook and other social networks as their primary communication. Thus, Facebook is an engagement hub.

In addition to knowing *where* to connect with Millennials, it is important to know how to motivate them at work. As members of the Trophy Generation, who earned their prize for merely participating in events, it should be of no surprise that they thirst for positive feedback, particularly from their manager. In fact, according to Barbara Keats, a management professor at the

W.P. Carey School of Business, "The Millennial generation craves compliments and constantly needs reassurance that they are performing well." In addition, accolades that can be noticed by their colleagues will pack twice the punch for them while public praise is also notably appreciated. However, like most other things in Millennials' lives, if the recognition is not posted on their social media "wall," it is almost as though it did not happen. Hence, this is another opportunity for Facebook.

Another effective means to motivate Millennial associates through external forces is through a respectful message from their manager. In many research studies conducted, "respect" was identified as the most important factor in reward and recognition programs. For a message to be respectful to Millennials, it must be credible, sincere and meaningful. It must also promote a *payoff* for the associate. For example, an effective message could be as simple as, "Your perseverance with this initiative is valued and will be rewarded."

Technology has also proven to be an effective motivator for Millennial associates. Technology presents organizations with the opportunity to reward associates with devices that make them feel special and recognize their talent by investing more in their hardware than the average associate's. In fact, technology has become completely unified into the everyday life of Millennials, as noted in a 2017 *Forbes* article. They no longer ask for sufficient technology at their jobs; they now *expect* it. Often, this expectancy has been painted as an entitlement, but what Millennial workers *really* want are the tools they need to do their job efficiently. For Millennials, such recognition and reward can spark enthusiasm in the job environment and generate indebted motivation within the associate. For instance, organizations should reward their highly regarded Millennial associates that have been assigned the top projects with the newest, fastest and lightest laptops available.

Legacy Hardware = Bad Morale

Please, don't give your Millennial workers that old Dell laptop that has been passed around the company for years. They want to be wowed by the newest, fastest, lightest devices you can offer.

In addition, if it does not provoke disruption among other associates, Millennials who are working on special projects (that require greater flexibility in terms of time and place) could be issued more portable, mobile devices as a reward (for their role) and a recognition (of the innovation required). For the crème of the crop Millennials, it may even behoove organizations to equip them with full-fledged mobile devices, such as smartphones or tablets, as a way to acknowledge their importance to the company. The aforementioned 2017 *Forbes* article also encourages companies to staff a "technology incubation team" with top-performing Millennials, in order to test new technology for their company and present findings to senior management. Regardless of position, it is vital for organizations to pay close attention to the hardware they issue to Millennials. In return, Millennials need to demonstrate that they can restrict the tools to professional use.

According to Cisco's "Connected World Technology Report", which surveyed Millennial associates across 14 countries, the ability to use superior hardware (laptop, tablet or smartphone) in the workplace will influence their job choice, sometimes even more than salary. As a matter of fact, 40 percent of Millennials surveyed said they would be willing to take a lower-paying job in exchange for better technology in the workplace.

The final consideration that is explored in this chapter as an external motivator for Millennials is the *cultural environment*. More specifically, flexible hours in the workplace and a collaborative group infrastructure have both demonstrated to be effective external motivators for the Millennial generation.

A Qualtrics study of Millennials (2017) found that, in exchange for a 3 percent pay cut, 77 percent would accept long term job security, 76 percent would accept flexible work hours and 67 percent would accept mentorship opportunities. If a larger 6 to 12 percent pay cut were required, these three percentages are still a meaningful 38 percent, 37 percent and 30 percent, respectively. At the same time, this Qualtrics study found that large minorities of Millennials would not accept a pay cut of any size to gain the benefits of working for a firm that only employs extremely talented and smart people (43 percent), is the market leader (41 percent) or has a fun office and casual culture (34 percent). Although money and income levels are important to Millennials, money (in and of itself) does *not* motivate them. Thus, the accumulation of money is not a goal for Millennials. Rather, they have a utilitarian perspective about money, whereby money is considered simply as a means to an end.

Similarly, Millennials also desire a team environment that promotes engagement. A Gallup study (2016) drew the disturbing conclusion that only 29 percent of Millennials feel engaged at work. In examining the benefits of an engagement culture and the risks of a non-engagement culture, this Gallup report found the business units in the top quartile of employee engagement are 17 percent more productive, suffer 70 percent fewer safety accidents, have 41 percent less absenteeism, experience 10 percent higher customer service ratings and are 21 percent more profitable than business units in the bottom quartile. As referenced in Chapter Eight, Millennials enjoy the social interaction among colleagues and do not mind sharing the glory of a successful project with a team. As a result, cultivating a work environment that instills "team work" will resonate well with Millennials eager to *bounce around* their ideas. Thus, it would behoove organizations to integrate flexible work hours in their workplace and facilitate collaborative work groups in their culture for Millennials when appropriate.

In summary, corporate reward and recognition programs are generally appreciated by all generations in the workplace. However, given their upbringing, it certainly appears that the Millennial generation is driven more by these externally driven programs than the prior cohorts in the workforce. Thus, organizational leaders must take the time to discern what is meaningful to each group, rather than follow hasty generalizations that typically do not cross generations. Likewise, it is the responsibility of the Millennial associates to help their respective organizational leaders to understand what is most important them. It is the intrinsic motivation within Millennials that has the ability to persist, regardless of any external factors. Hence, motivating the Millennials must be done from the inside out.

Chapter Eleven

Effective Leadership Styles
For Millennials

"Although they are better educated, more techno-savvy and quicker to adapt than those who have come before them, they refuse to blindly conform to traditional standards and time-honored institutions. Instead, they boldly ask, 'Why?'"

This quote from Eric Chester, author of *Employing Generation Why* describes the mindset of the Millennial generation with regard to their leadership. Based on the first 10 years of their workplace experience, it has become clear that Millennials desire to play an integral role with their employing organization, which requires an astute understanding of the big picture. As a result of this drive, Millennials have become known for asking more clarifying questions about their projects earlier in their careers than previous generations.

When this factor is considered with their predilection for a close relationship with their manager and craving for open communication in the workplace, it begs the question: "What organizational structure and leadership styles can effectively address these desires for Millennials in the workplace?" However, before these issues can be tackled, it is vital to articulate a general description of leadership for the context of this book. According to Jim Kouzes and Barry Posner, award-winning writers and researchers in leadership, when leaders understand that leadership is about "building a *relationship* by modeling the way, inspiring a shared vision, challenging the process, enabling others to act and encouraging the heart of their followers, they will be radically more effective at engaging employees."

Similarly, John Gardner, author of *On Leadership* says, "Leadership is the process of persuasion or example by which an individual or team induces a group to pursue goals held by a leader." James MacGregor Burns, another award-winning writer on leadership, also contends that leadership is meaningless without its connection to a common purpose.

Given this depiction of leadership and the Millennial generations' proclivities that are referenced in this chapter and throughout this book, which *organizational structure* is the most conducive within the workplace? The short answer is a flat design with minimal layers of hierarchy. A flat organizational structure lends itself to diminishing red tape and complication in management that hierarchical designs appear to be predisposed to, which has shown to significantly frustrate Millennial associates in numerous workplace studies. The "2015 Workplace Trends Report" by Randstad US found 83 percent of Millennials prefer working for a company with fewer layers of management. Because 91 percent in that same survey also indicated leadership aspirations, Millennials do not view a flatter structure as impeding their future leadership goals.

A flatter organization structure can also enable more empowerment for associates, a more effective and simpler communication process and an increased flexibility to cope with changing circumstances via more decentralized authority. These are all aspects that have been highly desired by Millennials in the workplace. Conversely, rigid, hierarchical structures will leave Millennials with a "stair case of bureaucracy" image that is daunting.

Although a hierarchical organizational design has shown to be especially effective in the U.S. military and within businesses when they are in crisis mode, it has also proven to limit the creativity of associates, which is one of the Millennials' greatest strengths. As a result, the nature of organizational leadership has evolved from a rigid, hierarchical model to a more empathetic, associate-focused style. Moreover, some organizations have developed Millennials creativity by infusing leadership practices that foster collaboration by providing associates a sense of personal involvement in the organization's operations.

Two other factors that lend themselves to a flatter organizational structure are the Millennial's aspiration for more collaboration via shared responsibility and decisions by consensus. While Millennials find it important to have areas of expertise, they have also expressed a penchant to weigh in on other areas of the organization. Case in point, in a quantitative study conducted by Intrepid, a world-renowned market research consultancy, with approximately 1,000 Millennial associates, the findings overwhelming indicated that Millennials believe (i.e. 82%) it is *important* to have a staff that can do each other's jobs.

Likewise, the majority (i.e. 54%) of Millennials in this research study preferred to make their decisions by "consensus." This percentage increases to 70% when Millennials are amongst their peers. Although most organizations are encouraged by the Millennials' teamwork-orientation, it does create some doubt about their ability to take responsibility for their actions, rather than simply ceding to a team without any personal accountability.

Hence, in order to alleviate this concern, it is imperative that the organizational structure is conducive to this objective. To that end, empirical studies have revealed that groups are more likely to advocate for personal accountability when the organizational design is *flat*.

Which *leadership styles* lend themselves to Millennial attributes and proclivities? Most generations, but especially Millennials, respond better to an Influential Leader style, rather than the harshly hierarchical, control and command approach previously discussed. The organizational leaders that have been "praised" by Millennials in the aforementioned studies appear to have a diligent understanding of the impact their personal and positional presence has on their ability to lead. Thus, they use influence to lead from the inside out.

Some of the essential attributes of an *influential leader* are their acute awareness of their core values and beliefs, the impact they have on others, their ability to make choices, how their communication style influences others, the power of their internal dialogue, what it takes to maintain a "work-life" balance, and the source of their unique personal strengths.

Given this template for success, what type of leadership styles can meet this expectation?

There is an array of leadership styles that range from management controlling the knowledge and skills *to* employees having the control. The illustration below depicts this range with 3 distinct leadership styles: Autocratic/Paternalistic, Participative/Democratic, and Delegative/Free Reign. Autocratic style says "I want both of you to…", Participative style says "Let's work together to…", and Delegative says "Take care of it while I go…".

Leadership Styles

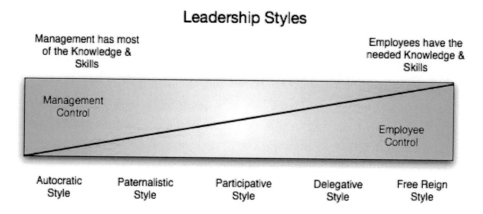

An autocratic style is used when leaders tell their associates what they want done and how it should be accomplished, without getting any input from their employees. This approach is effective when all the information to solve an issue is available, there is very little time to resolve a problem, and when the associates are well motivated. This style is often confused with an authoritarian approach, which is more abusive and unprofessional. The cartoon below is a depiction of the authoritarian style which "bosses people around."

"I don't like the opening essay. What's this stuff about the C.E.O. being 'a tragic figure whose leadership style is a reflection of his self-thwarted life, filled with yearning and disappointment'?"

The autocratic style is *not* an approach to which Millennials normally respond well. In fact, it has limited application for this generation given its incapacity for the Millennials' voice to be heard with this approach. An example of when it is appropriate is in training for a new position. In this instance, it can valuable when teaching a Millennial about a new skill set. However, the leader must be competent and a good coach for it to be effective. When the objective is to motivate the Millennial, a participative leadership style is more conducive.

A participative (or democratic) style involves the leader including their associates in the decision-making process (i.e., determining what to do and how to do it). As such, the leader maintains the final decision-making authority. However, they strongly involve their associates throughout the process up to the time a decision is made. This leadership approach is ideal for Millennial associates in the workplace given their overt desire to be involved earlier in their career and aspiration to have their voices heard. The illustration below portrays an image of the Millennial associates' predisposition to sharing feedback. At one time, this leadership style was considered a sign of weakness, particularly by the Silent generation. However, it is now regarded as a sign of respect and empathic strength.

105

This leadership style is typically used when the information necessary to complete the project is reliant on knowledge from the leader and the associates. Thus, this approach does not require the leader to know everything, which another reason why the Millennials are great candidates for this style given their well educated backgrounds and strong desire to be involved. Hence, this leadership style will be of mutual benefit as it allows the Millennials to be part of a team while empowering leaders to make more astute decisions.

With a delegative style, the leader empowers the associates to make the decisions. However, the leader is ultimately responsible for the final decisions that are made. This is primarily used when the leader is either unavailable or unable to accomplish an objective without support from associates. In these instances, the associates are able to analyze the situation and determine what needs to be done and how to do it. The leader is essentially responsible for setting priorities and delegating certain tasks. Given the Millennials desire to be provided direct guidance throughout the process, as well as their propensity to work under a mentor, this autonomous approach does not match up well with their disposition.

When Millennials are provided these "laissez faire" opportunities, it is imperative that the organizational leader provide explicit instructions, expectations and a prescriptive process to follow to prepare them for this approach.

Conversely, given their autonomous upbringing as latchkey kids, Gen X associates would feel well suited and comfortable with this leadership style. For organizational leaders, this is not a style to use so that they can blame others when things go wrong, rather an approach to be utilized when they fully trust and have confidence in the subordinates working on the assignment. An example of a situation that calls for delegative leadership with Millennials is a technological project. When the associates know more about an assignment than the leader, it is an opportunity to delegate a project to associates who are more capable of "doing" the project. This will allow the Millennial to contribute in a meaningful way and take ownership of the project.

An effective organizational leader will use all three of these styles, depending on what forces are interacting among the associate, the leader and the situation. Some forces that influence leadership style include: how much time is available, the relationship with the associate, internal conflicts, type of task, stress level and regulatory implications.

A different view, popularized by James MacGregor Burns, contrasts two styles of leadership: transactional and transformational. The transactional leadership style is based on transactions between leaders and followers. The basis of this method are transactions, such as rewards, punishment, reciprocity and exchanges (economic, emotional, physical). In other words, organizational leaders direct their associates by paying them and telling them what they need to do. As discussed in the prior chapter, Millennials tend to respond well to *extrinsic* rewards for motivation. Consequently, a rewards-based environment and leadership styles should drive strong results for Millennials given their craving for regular performance evaluations. However, this leadership style (in and of itself) is not sufficient.

In contrast, transformational leadership views the leader as one who can distill the values and needs of followers (i.e. associates) into a vision, then drives them to pursue it. Thus, a transformational leadership style influences the *intrinsic* motivation of associates, which makes it the ideal complement for a transactional leadership style. Moreover, in a 2010 survey that studied high-performing Millennials in the private and public sector, the transformational leadership style was ranked almost twice as high as a transactional style by associates (i.e. 4.31 versus 2.20 on a five-point scale). Hence, Millennials will clearly respond more favorably to a transformational leadership style than a transactional style.

Based on these studies and other research that is referenced throughout this book, a transformational leadership style is the proven approach in leading Millennial workers to realize their full potential while enabling an organization to achieve its mission as well. However, this does not mean that these two distinct styles are mutually exclusive. On the contrary, a hybrid style seems entirely plausible since transformational leadership builds on transactional leadership. This "augmented" approach is better known as collaboration.

A collaborative leadership style not only unites transactional and transformational approaches, but amalgamates servant leadership by selflessly placing emphasis on *others*. Thus, a collaborative leader will attempt to involve all stakeholders in an organization in leadership decisions. Consequently, a pitfall it will need to avoid is "overkill" in decision-making when it becomes too dependent on group consensus. As a result, in order for this team approach to be expeditious and effective, the organizational leader will need to step in when decisions get stalled in a group think impasse as strategies are discussed to death.

The collaborative leadership style has the following management characteristics:

- *Leading as peer problem solver* - The collaborative leader facilitates problem solving by modeling a process, and by helping others bring their experience and ideas to bear.
- *Building broad-based involvement* - The collaborative leader invites all stakeholders into an inclusive process, which detects problems or issues that need to be addressed.
- *Sustaining hope and participation* - The collaborative leader both helps the group set interim goals so it can see progress and pushes the group forward when matters arise.

A collaborative leadership approach also generally fosters close relationships among staff members, which facilitates more communication and cross-fertilization in their work, and leads them collectively to more effective methods to accomplish the organization's goals. Although it may be too soon to expect this team-oriented leadership style to make its way into Corporate America on a prominent scale, this approach is clearly tailor-made for the Millennial generation. Based on the aforementioned Millennial proclivity to play a more integral role in the workplace, aspiration for a closer relationships with their boss, and request for more open communications, a collaborative leadership style is the perfect combination that will meet these desires. Hence, perhaps it is time to consider trading the traditional boardroom table for a "round" table that aligns with this new leadership style.

Chapter Twelve

Leading a Multi-Generational Workforce

"If you provide employees an interesting job, good compensation, opportunities to learn and advance, colleagues they like to work with, a boss they trust, and leaders who are competent, associates of all generations will respond positively."

This quote from Jennifer Deal, author of *Retiring the Generation Gap*, portrays a consensus view shared by most generational research theorists and organizational leaders. This is obviously easier said than done. However, the real challenge is that this is the first time in modern U.S. history that we have four generations in the workforce at once. As a reminder, today's workforce consists of the following generations as defined in chapter 1: the Silent Generation (born between 1928 and 1945), Baby Boomers (born between 1946 and 1964), Gen Xers (born between 1965 and 1980), and Millennials (born between 1981 and 1996). Given each generation's unique attitudes, behaviors, expectations, motivations and habits, the organizational leader of today will not only need to adapt to the change in the composition of the workforce based on shifts in gender and ethnicity, but also need to reflect on the new generational differences that exist based on this diverse amalgamation.

With four distinct generations in the workplace, these unique differences (in how each conduct themselves) oblige a change. While the Silent generation workers continue to retire, Baby Boomers will remain the prominent majority in the workplace. In spite of the older cohort of this generation reaching "retirement age" (i.e. age 65), Baby Boomers have not left the workforce as expected. This dynamic is primarily attributed to the Great Recession from a few years ago. However, this also has to do with their desire to *die with their boots on*. In other words, unlike the previous (Silent) generation which is retiring as expected, Boomers are working longer and exiting the workforce slower than anticipated.

Preferences of Boomers, Gen Xers and Millennials, were captured in a Canadian survey conducted in 2017. The results, of which are summarized in the following chart:

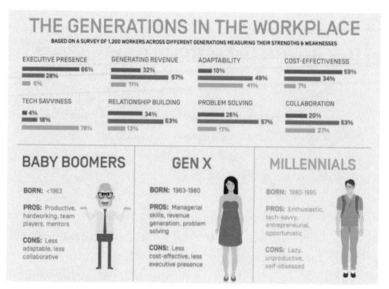

As of 2019, the vast majority of the Silent generation retired and oldest third of the Baby Boomers are now past normal retirement age. Millennial's historic growth and decline of generational workforce are highlighted in the following two 2017 Pew Research charts:

Millennials became the largest generation in the labor force in 2016

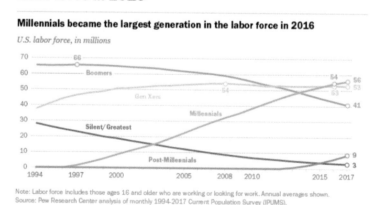

More than a third of the workforce are Millennials

% of the U.S. labor force

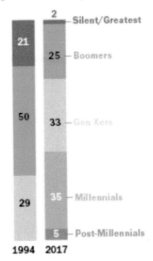

1994   2017

Note: Labor force includes those ages
16 and older who are working or looking
for work. Annual averages shown.
Source: Pew Research Center analysis
of monthly 1994 and 2017 Current
Population Survey (IPUMS).

PEW RESEARCH CENTER

In addition to the prior reasons cited, this rich mix of generations in the workforce can be attributed to labor shortages experienced in many industries and the rising average age of retirement. For instance, some organizations, especially in the healthcare industry, have revised their recruitment strategy to include retaining key associates past retirement age. While the pool of available workforce participants is larger than those who choose to participate, delays in retirement, improving nutrition and healthcare for those over age 65 and continued growth of the "gig economy" (more numerously available short term work opportunities, as discussed in the 2018 Deloitte Millennial Survey) may result in lasting workforce participation by Baby Boomers and the Silent Generation in the years ahead.

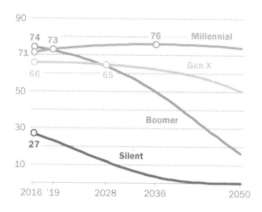

Projected population by generation

In millions

Note: Millennials refer to the population ages 20 to 35 as of 2016.
Source: Pew Research Center tabulations of U.S. Census Bureau population projections released December 2014 and 2016 population estimates.

PEW RESEARCH CENTER

Hence, although the Silent generation's exodus can be planned, the same can't be said for the Baby Boomer generation, which may stick around for some time. As a result, organizational leaders will need to take both of these variables into consideration as they plan for, manage, and lead their multi-generational workforce. Managing associates from numerous generations is not an easy task, but it is a reality of the business world today. In order to truly build a cohesive workplace, leaders must encourage their associates to view generational differences as a valuable strength to the organization rather than a weakness.

In order to accommodate all these generations that are currently in the workplace, an effective leader recognizes their associate's preferences on matters (such as, how they desire to be managed, communicated with and obtain feedback) and subsequently weighs these issues to assure they can align with their organization's mission, vision and culture. Hence, what are the "distinctions" for each of these matters in each of these generations?

For the Silent generation, managers that drive them crazy tend to be too "touchy-feely," are indecisive, worry about making unpopular decisions, use excessive profanity and are disorganized. For Boomers, managers that irritate them are not open to input, are bureaucratic, send a "my-way-or-the-highway" message, are apathetic and practice one-upmanship. For Gen Xers, managers that frustrate them micro-manage, do not walk the talk, spend too much time on process and too little on results and are bureaucratic. For Millennials, managers that exasperate them are condescending, treat them as if they are too young to be valuable, are cynical and sarcastic, seem threatened by technology and are unreliable and disorganized. The empirical studies that validated these observations were primarily conducted by Dr. Susan Murphy (business consultant with Claire Raines Associates) in conjunction with AARP.

Another clear distinction among these generations is how they view their work career. According to research conducted by generational experts in the book "Millennial Leaders," the Silent generation prefers the traditional career path, which creates a stigma for job changers. Conversely, Boomers view their career as a 60-hour work week, which involves paying your dues and changing jobs as a "waste of time." On the contrary, Gen Xers prefer job flexibility in the workplace (e.g.., the four-day workweek), while viewing changing jobs as potentially necessary in order to achieve their eventual career growth.

On the other hand, Millennials have made it clear through their behaviors outlined in this book that they desire multiple careers and generous flexibility in the workplace. In this aforementioned research, Millennials viewed job changing as normal, with a norm of two to three years in a position. In addition, they expressed aspirations to own a business outside of full-time work. In order to attain this objective, Millennials seek flexible hours from their employer that permit working from home since they are "always connected."

POTENTIAL GENERATIONAL CONFLICT

Traditionals & Boomers

- Experience-focused
- Activity-based
- Belief in youth's potential
- Measured Risk (i.e change wary)
- Understand role of politics (vertical based)
- In-person communication

CULTURE COLLISION

Gen X & Gen Y

- Competency-focused
- Facts and results driven
- Believe they have arrived
- Risk-takers (i.e. trial & error)
- Suspicious of politics (horizontal based)
- Wireless, instant communications

Given these contrasts, it should be of no surprise to an organizational leader why there seems to be such a disconnect with potential generational conflicts as illustrated by this graphic. Moreover, this comparison highlights additional discord that exists between generations, particularly among younger and older cohorts. Thus, organizational leaders should consider these validated observations and avoid these "landmines" when possible.

Another distinction that is evident in the workplace between these generations is the frequency of feedback they aspire to receive from their managers. More specifically, the Silent generation predominantly lives by the mantra "no feedback is good feedback," Boomers expect to receive feedback (once a year) on their annual performance reviews, Gen Xers seek feedback from their colleagues but not necessarily from authority figures and Millennials insist on receiving feedback from their manager as frequently as possible.

In addition to understanding these generational differences, it is equally important to comprehend *why* they clash. It ultimately comes down to each generation's upbringing which develops their cultural lens (i.e., perspective based on their experiences). A notable example when this is evident is a family get-together or vacation. For instance, it usually does not take long for someone from the older generations to reference the good old days or younger generation to roll their eyes when they try to imagine not having the Internet. A business example of this disconnect is personified with investing in the stock market. For instance, the Silent generation still recalls the damaging effect the stock market crash had on their daily life, where as the Boomers only have the remnants of the conversations to truly understand this perspective. Likewise, Millennials experienced the first 10 years of their investment lives in a secular bear market that is still recovering, where as the Gen Xers started their investment experience with the strongest bull market run in our history.

Thus, generational conflict is one of the last bastions of acceptable discrimination in today's workplace. Consequently, it would behoove organizational leaders to carefully consider the implications of their decisions before acting on their "gut" feeling, which is likely tainted by their own cultural lens and bias. Likewise, it would behoove associates from all generations to take these insights into consideration before judging their peers.

Some other generational challenges that organizational leaders encounter include distinct perspectives on work ethic, authority and relationships. These differences, which are illustrated by the chart below, can cause conflict, frustration and misunderstandings if they are not managed well. Hence, these are key factors that will influence the workplace. The research and insights from the chart above were deducted from a 2013 DBA Docket article titled, "How Will Millennials Transform the Future of Law?"

Differences in the Workplace

	Traditionalists	Baby Boomers	Generation X	Millennials
Outlook	Practical	Optimistic	Skeptical, Individualistic	Hopeful and Optimistic
Work Ethic	Loyal, Sacrifice	Driven	Balanced	Eager but anxious
Value in Workplace	Similarity (melting pot)	Profitability, reputation	Stimulation, autonomy	Diversity, structure, relationships
Views on Authority	Chain of Command	Change of Command	Self-Command	Don't Command – Collaborate
Views on Leadership	By Hierarchy	By Consensus	By Competence	By Pulling Together
Feedback	No news is good news	Once a year with documentation	Periodic with 360 degrees	Impersonal at touch of button
Time at Work is Defined As	Punch clock	Visibility	Why does it matter if I get it done at 2 a.m.?	Is it 5 p.m.? I have a life.
Communication	Formal (Memo) or Face-to-face	Telephone	Email	IM/Texting, Social Networking
Preferred Learning Method	Expert	Expert	From each other	Group, interactive, technology
Motivated By	Respect for Experience	Achievement	Do it Your Way	Collaboration

To that end, organizational leaders should set time aside to learn how their various team members wish to communicate together at the beginning of any team formation. For teams already in place, the organizational leader should create a cultural and coordinating program that fosters communication and collaboration between the present generations in the workforce. This effort should help to alleviate some of these challenges and conflicts.

It is also beneficial for organizational leaders to have a common understanding for each generation's communication preferences. Although it is always perilous to make any broad assumption that indicts a whole generation (or any group, for that matter), having a more perceptive comprehension for their proclivities should help organizational leaders to more effectively relate to and empathize with their associates. For instance, it is helpful for organizational leaders to know that associates from the Silent generation prefer "face-to-face" conversations that contain words and a tone of voice that is respectful, has clear diction, and bars slang. In other words, these associates respond better when the language is formal, professional, and the message relates to company history and long-term goals.

For Boomers, the conversation between an organizational leader and an associate should be more relational and personal (perhaps over coffee or lunch). Boomers also tend to perceive relationship and business results as intertwined with personalized connections (i.e. How is your daughter doing in school?). Hence, it would behoove the organizational leader to make their conversations participative by soliciting their input and subsequently linking the message to the organization's values. In contrast, when conversing with Gen X associates, organizational leaders should be direct, straight-forward, and avoid wasting their time with corporate-speak. For instance, when communicating a message to them, either leave them a voice mail (or if necessary an e-mail) that clearly states what to do, when it is needed, and how it will serve the Gen Xer. Conversely, when communicating with Millennial associates, an organizational leader should be positive and avoid scorn. The message should be transmitted face-to-face or via a text message (depending on the circumstance – see chapters 3, 4 and 8 in this manuscript for more specific instructions). Moreover, it should tie back to personal goals or the goals their team is working toward. Although there is clearly merit in discovering and addressing crucial differences between generational workers, it is also beneficial to discern the important commonalities in order to find common ground to bridge them. Successful organizations find ways to "leverage" these similarities to ensure their leaders not only understand these connections, but create a work environment to support them. Some commonalities which appear to be universal in nature across all generational associates in today's American workforce are as follows:

1. **Work is viewed as a vehicle for personal fulfillment and satisfaction** – work is *not* just a paycheck is a cross-generational mantra. Having said that though, it is also clear that workers by and large want compensation that's commensurate with their industry.

2. **Workplace culture is important to the job satisfaction of associates** – the "highest" indicator of job satisfaction for associates of all generations is to feel *valued* on the job.

3. **Rewarding work environment is paramount** – more than 70% of associates in the workforce want a supportive environment where they are recognized and appreciated.

4. **Career development is a high priority** – although three-quarters of organizations rate this highly, only half of employees give their employer good marks in this area.

5. **Flexibility is important** – more than 70% of all associates in the workforce across all generations would like to be able to set their own hours, as long as the work gets done.

These generational insights are attributed to research conducted by Randstad corporation, a global, temporary employment company specializing in flexible work and HR services.

Based on these "commonly held" beliefs across all generations in the workforce and previously referenced findings, 3 rules of engagement for organizational leaders are:

1. **Use Clear, Straightforward Language** - some senior management, particularly from the Silent and Boomer generation, will speak in generalities when giving directives to associates. These directives are often confused as *suggestions* by the younger cohorts.

2. **Don't Assume Anything** – organizational leaders need to spell out what they want to be done by their associates. A "hinting" strategy (that is not explicit) may have been effective with Boomers and the Silent generation, but could be perceived as a "silly" game by younger associates that are expecting to be told *exactly* what they should do.

3. **When an Employee Gets It Right, Celebrate!** – the Silent generation celebrates their retirement, Boomers their promotion, but Gen X and Millennials celebrate everything.

The right combination of policies and best practices is the "key" to a productive, engaged, and generational-neutral workforce. Organizations that are highly successful at managing a multi-generational workforce have accomplished this honor by adopting best practices that amend their workplace culture, benefit options and compensation plans to a version that takes all generations into account. Some examples of these best practices are:

• **Workplace Culture:** The first step involves studying the generational composition of the workforce. However, according to a Conference

Board survey, only a third of companies have taken this essential step. Second, facilitate regular conversations about generational differences to increase appreciation for diversity and cultivate respect for all generations. Third, create a work environment where all associate opinions are valued. Lastly, match the generational composition of your workforce with your customer base to enable them to be aligned with people that have similar interests and relate to them more effectively.

- **Benefit Option Recommendations:** The first step is to offer flexible work options where available. Keep in mind that not all business units lend themselves to this structure so this should only be used when it is not disruptive to the organization. Second, offer a menu of benefits for associates that match to their needs, rather than a "one-size-fits-all" approach.
- **Compensation Recommendations:** The first step is make sure your program rewards an associate's performance and productivity, not just time on the job. A "good" system will encourage and reward productivity regardless of age. Second, present a strong employer-match savings plan, especially for associates nearing retirement. Likewise, offer younger associates programs that pay off their student loans (see chapters 6 and 9 for more detail). Generational research by author, Howard Munson, validated many of these best practices.

The final step that is particularly necessary to lead a multi-generational workforce is "empowering" your respective generational worker. Like the previous aspects, this task will also need to be distinct for each generation in order to attain maximum effectiveness. Based on workshops developed through five years of academic, sociological research, as well as various books, periodicals, and professional journals, Jeff Vargas (Chief Learning Officer for the United States Department of Energy) unveiled these subsequent findings:

- The most effective technique to "empower" the Silent generation is by making time for personal relations, demonstrating respect for history and tradition, embracing hallmarks of family values and good manners, being linear and logical by emphasizing applicable facts, creating occasions to socialize, and honoring hard work with formal recognition.
- The most effective technique to "empower" *Baby Boomers* is by asking for their input and expertise, allowing them ways to build consensus, giving them public recognition and rewards for their work, providing them perks

in line with their professional status, and placing them in charge of key projects that will demonstrate their leadership savvy.

- The most effective technique to "empower" *Gen Xers* is by allowing them to prioritize projects as they see fit, providing regular feedback (constructive and critical), creating opportunities for fun at work, utilizing the latest technology, encouraging their pursuit of interests outside of work, and providing them perks that reward their contributions.
- The most effective technique to "empower" *Millennials* is by encouraging autonomy, diversity, communications, teamwork, openness to ideas, and respect, keeping up with their (fast) pace, acting like a coach, promoting in-house education, providing state-of-the-art resources, offering challenging assignments that play a key role, and involving them in a partnership (i.e. solicit their ideas and feedback, work with them as a team).

Ultimately, all generational workers will need to make some sacrifice for the good of their organization in order to account for the *Millennial shift*. For the Silent generation, they will need to adjust to the new demand for customization, as well as provide wisdom, mentoring and leadership to Millennials. For Boomers, they will need to give up the need to constrain Millennials, as well as prepare them so they can eventually pass the baton. For Gen Xers, they will need to give up their need for independence and start dedicating themselves to guiding the Millennials by demonstrating their confidence and teamwork. For Millennials, they will need to shift from social networks to face-to-face community networks, as well as use their knowledge to improve efficiency and create social change.

By the end of the next decade, Millennials may not be CEOs of every Fortune 500 company - probably not even the majority of them. But Millennials like Mark Zuckerberg (Facebook), David Karp (Tumbler), James Park (Fitbit) and Marissa Mayer (Yahoo), will continue to change the methods we communicate with, consume media, browse the web, and make products. In order to succeed, organizations will need to have Millennial values sewn into the fabric of their companies. Hence, organizations will need to strive to find new techniques to empower this innovative generation and unlock their creativity as they advocate for change. Consequently, it is crucial for organizational leaders to understand that the generational balance of the workplace is in fact shifting and Millennials will be key to successful adaptation.

In order to work effectively and efficiently, to increase productivity and quality, organizational leaders need to understand generational characteristics, and learn how to use them profitably for their organization's benefit. These aforementioned strategies can find the common ground necessary to bridge the multi-generational gap in the workforce.

REFERENCES

AllThingsMillennial. "Gen-happy." *AllThingsMillennial* (blog), July 20, 2009. http://allthingsmillennial.wordpress.com/tag/millennial/.

Alsop, Ron. *The Trophy Kids Grow Up: How the Millennial Generation is Shaking up the Workplace*. San Francisco: Jossey-Bass, 2008.

Anthony, Mitch. *The New Retirementality*. Chicago: Dearborn, 2001.

Association for Talent Development. "Long-Term Business Success can Hinge on Succession Planning." *ATD* (formerly *Training Directors'*) *Forum Newsletter* 5, 1989.

Auby, Karen. "A Boomer's Guide to Communicating with Gen X and Gen Y." *Business Week*, Aug. 14, 2008.

Baby Boomer Headquarters. "The Boomer Stats." *Baby Boomer Headquarters*, 2008. http://www.bbhq.com/ bomrstat.htm.

Baker, Wayne. "Generation Y or Millennials: Optimistic or unrealistic?" *The Ann Arbor News,* Feb. 23, 2011.

Bannon, Shele, Kelly Ford, and Linda Meltzer. "Understanding Millennials in the Workplace." *CPA Journal*, Nov. 1, 2011.

Bell, Chip. *Managers as Mentors: Building Partnerships for Learning*. New York: Berrett-Koehler, 2002.

Black, J. Steward, Allen J. Morrison, and Hal B. Gregersen. *Global Explorers: The Next Generation of Leaders*. New York: Routledge, 1999.

Boisvert, Trisha Gallagher. "When Structuring Mentor Programs, Consider the Benefits in Both Directions." *Society of Financial Service Professionals Leadership & Management*, Nov. 2008.

Bower, Joseph L. "Solve the Succession Crisis by Growing Inside-Outside Leaders." *Harvard Business Review*, Nov. 2007.

Bradley, Alexandra. "The Time has Come to Embrace Millennial Perspectives." *TD* (formerly *T+D) Magazine*, 2010.

Burkus, David. "Developing the Next Generation of Leaders: How to Engage Millennials in the Workplace." *Leadership Advance Online*, 2010. http://www.regent.edu/acad/global/publications/lao/issue_19/Burkus_leading_next_generation.pdf.

Burns, James MacGregor. *Leadership*. New York: Harper Collins, 1985

ByAllAccounts. "Social Media Marketing 101 for Financial Advisors." *Social Media Webinar*, 2011.

Caner, Mark E. "Spiritual Meekness: An Imperative Virtue for Christian Leaders." *Inner Resources for Leaders* 2, no. 3: 1-9, 2010.

Caner, Mark E. 2009. "Building Your Bench Strength." *Society of Financial Service Professionals Leadership & Management*, Feb. 2009.

Charan, Ram. "Ending the CEO Succession Crisis." *Harvard Business Review*, March 2005.

Chester, Eric. *Employing Generation Why?* Vacaville, CA: Chess Press, 2012.

Chrislip, David D., and Carl E. Larson. *Collaborative Leadership: How Citizens and Civic Leaders Can Make a Difference*. San Francisco: Jossey Bass, 1995.

Cisco. "Air, Food, Water, Internet – Cisco Study Reveals Just How Important Internet and Networks Have Become as Fundamental Resources in Daily Life." *Cisco Newsroom*, Sept. 21, 2011. http://newsroom.cisco.com/press-release-content?type=webcontent&articleId=474852.

Cohen, Emily. "Managing a Cross-Generational Creative Team" (Presentation). InHOWse Conference, Jan. 12, 2012.

Cohn, Fred. "The New Age of Leadership." *UniversumGlobal.com*, June 9, 2011. http://www.employerbrandingtoday.com/blog/2011/06/09/the-new-age-of-leadership/.

College Board, The. "Trends in College Pricing 2011." *CollegeBoard.org*, 2011. http://trends.collegeboard.org/.

Collins, Jim. *Good to Great*. New York: HarperCollins, 2001.

Covey, Stephen R. *The 7 Habits of Highly Effective People*. New York: Fireside, 1989.

Conger, Cristen. "Don't Blame Facebook for the Narcissism Epidemic." *Discovery News*, Aug. 4, 2010. http://news.discovery.com/tech/dont-blame-facebook-narcissism-epidemic-110804.html.

Crandell, Susan. "How To Be a Leader In the Digital Age." *NBCUniversal*, March 5, 2012. http://work.lifegoesstrong.com/article/how-be-leader-digital-age.

DBH Consulting. "Is Your Leadership Style Encouraging or Discouraging Your Next Generation of Leaders?" *DBH Consulting* (blog), Dec. 21, 2011. http://www.dbhconsulting.com/blog/Is_Your_Leadership_Style_Encouraging_or_Discouraging/.

Deal, Jennifer J., David G. Altman, and Steven G. Rogelberg. "Millennials at Work: What We Know and What We Need to Do (If Anything)." *Journal Of Business & Psychology*, June 2010.

Deal, Jennifer J. *Retiring the Generation Gap: How Employees Young and Old Can Find Common Ground*. San Francisco: Jossey-Bass, 2006.

Degraffenreid, Scott. "Millennials Language and Lifestyle: Text Speak - Text Life." *Millennial Issues*, 2010. http://wedidthemath.com/articles/ m_article_sd08.08.php.

Delcampo, Robert G., Lauren A. Haggerty, Meredith Jane Haney, and Lauren Ashley Knippel. *Managing the Multi-Generational Workforce*. Burlington, VT: Gower, 2011.

Digest of Education Statistics, National Center for Education Statistics, U.S. Department of Education Institute of Education Sciences, http://nces.ed.gov/program/digest/d08

DMW Direct Reports. *Millennials: The Gen Y Tsunami is Here*. Chesterbrook, PA: DMW Direct Reports, 2010.

Doublestein, Barry. "The Genesis of Values: A Christian Perspective." *Leader-Values.com*, 2006. http://www.leader-values.com/Content/detail. asp?ContentDetailID=1146.

Dugas, Christine. "Generation Y's steep financial hurdles: Huge debt, no savings." *USA Today*, April 26, 2010.

Dychtwald, Ken. *Age Power: How the 21st Century will be Ruled by the New Old*. New York: Tarcher, 2000.

Dyck, B., M. Mauws, F.A. Starke, and G.A. Mischke. "Passing the baton: the importance of sequence, timing, technique and communication in executive succession." *Journal of Business Venturing, 17*, 2002.

Edgewalk Business Experience. *How Millennials Communicate Socially vs. Professionally*. Bellevue, WA: Edgewalk Business Experience, 2011.

Employer's Resource Council. "What's most important to the Millennials?" *Where Great Workplaces Start* (blog), 2008. http://greatworkplace. wordpress.com/2008/03/11/whats-most-important-to-the-millennials/.

Epstein, Molly, and Polly Howes. "The Millennial Generation: Recruiting, Retaining and Managing." *Today's CPA*, Sept./Oct., 2006.

Espinoza, Chip, Mick Ukleja, and Craig Rusch. *Managing the Millennials: Discover the Core Competencies for Managing Today's Workforce.* Hoboken, NJ: Wiley, 2010.

Ethics Resource Center. "2011 National Business Ethics Survey: Workplace Ethics in Transition." *Ethics & Compliance Initiative*, 2012. http://www.ethics.org/nbes/files/FinalNBES-web. pdf.

Ethics Resource Center. "Millennials, Gen X and Baby Boomers: Who's Working at Your Company and What Do They Think About Ethics?" *Ethics & Compliance Initiative*, Nov. 18, 2009. http://www.ethics.org/resource/2009-national-business-ethics-survey/.

Fields, Bea, Scott Wilder, Jim Bunch, and Rob Newbold. *Millennial Leaders: Success Stories from Today's Most Brilliant Generation & Leaders.* Buchanan, NY: Pubmatch, 2008.

Gardner, John William. *On Leadership.* New York: Free Press, 1993.

Gibbs, Nancy. "How Millennials Perceive a New Generation Gap." *Time*, March 11, 2010.

Green Buzz Agency. "Marketing Psychographics – Talkin' Bout My Generation." *GreenBuzz* (blog), Aug. 10, 2010. http://www.greenbuzzagency.com/marketing-demographics-talkin%E2%80%99-%E2%80%98bout-my-generation.

Greenleaf, Robert. *Servant Leadership: A Journey into the Nature of Legitimate Power and Greatness.* Mahwah, NJ: Paulist Press, 1983.

Gupta, Ashim. "Motivating the Millennials." *Practical-Management.com*, May 17, 2011. http://www.practical-management.com/Organization-Development/Motivating-the-Millennials.html.

Hammill, Greg. "Mixing and Managing Four Generations of Employees." *FDU Magazine*, Winter/Spring 2005.

Harrington, Michael. "Millennials: Engage, Motivate, and Retain the New Workforce." *New Directions*, 2005. http://www.newdirectionsconsulting.com/pdfs/Millennials_Engage_Motivate_and_Retain_the_New_Workforce.pdf.

Hartman, Jackie L., and Jim McCambridge. "Optimizing Millennials' Communication Styles." *Business Communication Quarterly*, 2011.

Hartwell, Sharalyn. "Are you fluent in the Millennial language?" *Generation Y Examiner*, April 5, 2010. http://www.examiner.com/generation-y-in-national/are-you-fluent-the-millennial-language/.

Haserot, Phyllis. "Different generations in the workplace can collaborate successfully." *AccountingWEB*, Aug. 20., 2009. http://www.accountingweb.com/topic/education-careers/different-generations-workplace-can-collaborate-successfully.

Hassler, Christine. "Are 20-Somethings Naively Optimistic About Their Careers?" *The Huffington Post*, Jan. 28, 2011. http://www.huffingtonpost.com/ christine-hassler/20-somethings-careers_b_814788.html.

Heathfield, Susan M. "Managing Millennials: Eleven Tips for Managing Millennials." About.com, 2012. http://humanresources.about.com/od/managementtips/a/millenials.htm.

Herbison, Gerry, and Glenn Boseman. "Here They Come – Generation Y. Are You Ready?" *Journal of Financial Service Professionals*, May, 2009.

Hershatter, Andrea, and Molly Epstein. "Millennials and the World of Work: An Organization and Management Perspective." *Journal Of Business & Psychology*, 2010.

Hewlett, Sylvia Ann, Laura Sherbin, and Karen Sumberg. "How Gen Y & Boomers Will Reshape Your Agenda." *Harvard Business Review*, July 2009.

Hobart, Buddy, and Herb Sendek. *Gen Y Now: How Generation Y Changes Your Workplace and Why It Requires a New Leadership Style*. Novato, CA: Select Press, 2009.

Hoffer, Steven. "Google+ Fastest Growing Social Network Ever, ComScore Study Says." *The Huffington Post*, Aug. 3, 2011. http://www.huffingtonpost.com/2011/ 08/03/google-plus-fastest-growing-social_n_917389.html.

House, Robert J., and Mansour Javidan. *Culture, Leadership and Organizations: The GLOBE Study of 62 Societies*. Thousand Oaks, CA: Sage, 2004.

Howe, Neil. *Millennials in the Workplace: Human Resource Strategies for a New Generation*. Great Falls, VA: LifeCourse Associates, 2010.

Hunter, James. *The Servant: A Simple Story about the True Essence of Leadership*. New York: Crown, 1998.

IDG Connect. *iPad for Business: Survey 2012*. Framingham, MA, 2012.

Javidan, Mansour. "Understanding and Managing Cultural Issues" (Presentation). Regent University, Virginia Beach, VA, 2008.

Kachaner, Nicolas, and Michael S. Deimler. "How Leading Companies are Stretching Their Strategy." *Strategy and Leadership,* 2008.

Kouzes, James M., and Barry Z. Posner. *The Leadership Challenge.* San Francisco: Jossey-Bass, 1987.

Kramer, Larry. "The Globe: How French Innovators Are Putting the 'Social' Back in Social Networking." *Harvard Business Review* 88, Oct. 2010.

Kuykendall, Lavonne. "Advisers warm up to Twitter, give cold shoulder to cold calling: Increasingly, social media the choice for reaching out to prospects." *Investment News,* April 6, 2011.

Lackey, James E., Kamena, Gene, and Paul Calvert. "Millennials and Transformational leaders: A Winning Team for the Future." *The Free Library,* 2010. http://www.thefreelibrary.com/Millennials: and transformational leaders: a winning team for the...-a0247037934.

Lancaster, Lynne C., and David Stillman. *The M-factor: How the Millennial Generation is Rocking the Workplace.* New York: Harper Business, 2010.

Levenson, Alec R. "Millennials and the World of Work: An Economist's Perspective." *Journal Of Business & Psychology,* 2010.

LIMRA. *Marketing to Generation Y: Messages that Get Their Attention.* Windsor, CT, 2009.

LIMRA. *Understanding the Web Link: Gen X, Gen Y, and Life Insurance.* Windsor, CT, 2010.

Lipken, Nicole A., and April J. Perrymore. *Y in the Workplace: Managing the 'Me First' Generation.* Franklin Lakes, NJ: Career Press, 2009.

LL Global. 2011. *The Cutting Edge: Where the Next Generation of Sales Talent Meets Today's Industry Needs.* Windsor, CT, 2011.

Loden, Marilyn, and Judy Rosener. *Workforce America: Managing Employee Diversity as a Vital Resource.* New York: McGraw-Hill, 1990.

Madden, Kaitlin. "Will Millennials always be preceded by their reputation at work?" *Career Builder,* March 30, 2011. http://www.theworkbuzz.com/careers/millennials-preceded-by-reputation-at-work/.

Maffin, Tod. "Top five reasons Generation Y workers leave their employer." *Emily Carr University of Art + Design* (blog), 2009. http://blogs.eciad.ca/elverum/2009/08/19/top-five-reasons-generation-y-workers-leave-their-employer/

Mandell, Nancy R. "SEC Doesn't 'Like' Facebook." *Financial Planning Magazine,* Jan. 31, 2012.

Marston, Cam. *Motivating the 'What's in it for Me?' Workforce*. Hoboken, NH: Wiley, 2007.

Mehrabian, Albert, and Susan R. Ferris. "Inference of Attitude from Nonverbal Communication in Two Channels." *The Journal of Counseling Psychology 31*, 1967.

Meister, Jeanne C., and Karie Willyerd. *The 2020 Workplace: How Innovative Companies Attract, Develop, and Keep Tomorrow's Employees Today*. New York: HarperCollins, 2010.

Mr. Youth, and Intrepid. "What your company will look like when Millennials call the shots." *Millennial Inc.* Chelsea Market. White Paper, 2011.

Murphy, Susan A. "Leading a Multigenerational Workforce." *AARP The Magazine*, 2007.

Myers, Karen, and Kamyab Sadaghiani. "Millennials in the Workplace: A Communication Perspective on Millennials' Organizational Relationships and Performance." *Journal Of Business & Psychology 25,* 2010.

Notter, Jamie. "Moving Beyond the Hype about Generational Diversity." *Journal Of Association Leadership*, Fall 2007.

Ogbonna, Emmanuel, and Lloyd C. Harris. "Organizational Culture: It's not what you think." *Journal of General Management 23*, 1998.

Overfelt, Maggie. "Millennial employees are a lot more loyal than their job-hopping stereotype." *CNBC.com.*, May 10, 2017. https://www.cnbc.com/2017/05/10/90-of-millennials-will-stay-in-a-job-for-10-years-if-two-needs-met.html.

Palser, Barb. "Beneath the Tattoos." *American Journalism Review*, June/July 2010.

Parker-Pope, Tara. "Time to Review Workplace Reviews?" *The New York Times*, May 17, 2010.

PBS. "Generation jobless: Millennials struggle with unemployment." (A. Leonard, Producer). *PBS.org,* Oct. 7, 2010. http://www.pbs.org/wnet/need-to-know/ economy/generation-jobless-millennials-struggle-with-unemployment/4127/.

Pfeffer, Jeffrey. *The Human Equation*. Boston: Harvard Press, 1998.

Pew Research Center. "Millenials: A Portrait of Generation Next." *Pew Research Center*, 2010.

Phillips, Carol. "Mobile Millennials Leading the Way." *MillennialMarketing. com*, Oct. 15, 2010. http://millennialmarketing.com/2010/10/mobile -millennials-leading-the-way/.

Potter, Ned. "Facebook IPO: $5 Billion Filing to Sell Stock in May." *ABC News*, Feb. 1, 2012.

Qualtrics. "Work ReMixed." *The Millennial Study*, 2017. https://www.qualtrics. com/millennials/.

Rabinowitz, Phil. "Styles of Leadership." *Community Tool Box*, 2012. http://ctb. ku.edu/en/tablecontents/sub_section_main_1122.aspx.

Rainer, Thom S., and Jess W. Rainer. *The Millennials: Connecting to America's Largest Generation*. Nashville: B&H Publishing Group, 2011.

Ready, Douglas A., and Jay A. Conger. "Make Your Company a TALENT FACTORY." *Harvard Business Review 85*, 2007.

Reisinger, Don. "Engaging Millennial IT Workers: Rethink Everything." *CIO Insight*, Aug. 30, 2010.

Reith, J. "Understanding and Appreciating the Communication Styles of the Millennial Generation." *American Counseling Association*, 2005. http:// www.counselingoutfitters.com/ vistas/vistas05/Vistas05.art70.pdf.

Robert Half International. "What Millennial Workers Want: How to Attract and Retain Gen Y Employees." *Robert Half International*, 2008. http:// www.accountingweb-cgi.com/ whitepapers/generationy_robert_half.pdf.

Rorholm, Janet. "Generational Gap Changes Roles for Employees." *Knight Ridder Tribune Business News*, Sept. 24, 2007.

Rose, Joni. "Learning style and values of Generation Y." *TheSalesFeed*, April 14, 2007. http://trainingpd.suite101.com/article.cfm/designing_training_for _gen_y.

Rothwell, William J. *Effective Succession Planning: Ensuring Leadership Continuity and Building Talent from Within*. New York: AMACOM, 2005.

Rubesch, Heather. "The Millenials Are Here!!! Are You Relevant?" *Savvy B2B Marketing*, June 30, 2010. http://www.savvyb2bmarketing.com/blog/ entry/780151/the-millenials-are-here-are-you-relevant.

Schwartz, Dana. "Report on Millennials: Young, Underemployed and Optimistic." *Come Recommended* (blog), Feb. 20, 2012. http:// comerecommended. com/blog/2012/02/20/report-on-millennials-young -underemployed-optimistic/#.

Seaton, Deborah. "Emoticons, text-speak pop up in emails." *The South End*, Nov. 11, 2011. http://thesouthend.wayne.edu/index.php/article/2011/11/emoticons_textspeak_pop_up_in_emails#comment1458.

Shaik, Pervin. "Managing Gen Y in Today's Workplace: The Positive Impact of a New Generation of Employees." *Suite 101*, July 31, 2009. http://pervinshaikh.suite101.com/managing-young-talent-in-21st-century-workplace-a135784.

Shandler, Donald. *Motivating the Millennial Knowledge Worker.* Fairport, NY: Axzo Press, 2009.

Sharp, Kelly. "Gen Y- the employee of the future: How Generation Y will benefit and challenge managers." *Suite 101*, July 3, 2009. http://employee-management-relations.suite101.com/article.cfm/gen_y_the_employee_of_the_future.

Smith, Molly. "Managing Generation Y as they change the workforce." *Reuters*, Jan. 8, 2008.

Solis, Brian. *Engage!: The Complete Guide for Brands and Businesses to Build, Cultivate, and Measure Success in the New Web.* Hoboken, NJ: Wiley, 2011.

Solomon, Rachel. "Running a Business: Learning to Manage Millennials." *The Wall Street Journal*, March 15, 2008.

Sujansky, Joanne G., and Jan Ferri-Reed. *Keeping the Millennials: Why Companies are Losing Billions in Turnover to this Generation.* Hoboken, NJ: Wiley, 2009.

Taraci, Tom. (2012, March 7). "Facebook Is The Secret To Motivating Millennial Workers." *All Facebook*, March 7, 2012. http://www.allfacebook.com/facebook-millennials-2012-03.

Thielfoldt, Diane, and Devon Scheef. "Generation X and The Millennials: What You Need to Know About Mentoring the New Generations." *Law Practice Today*, Aug. 2004.

Tulgan, Bruce. *Not Everyone Gets a Trophy: How to Manage Generation Y.* San Francisco: Jossey-Bass, 2009.

Turner, Gregory. "Understanding Generation X ... Boom or bust introduction." *All Business*, Dec. 25, 2005. http://www.allbusiness.com/ marketing/direct-marketing/620473-1.html.

Van Riper, Tom. "Text-message generation entering workplace." *Forbes*, Aug. 30, 2006.

Vargas, Jeffrey. "Understanding and Working with Generational Differences" (Presentation). LULAC Conference, Cincinnati, OH, June 28, 2011.

Wells Fargo Asset Management. "2017 Millennial Survey: Uniting Happiness and Money." *Wells Fargo*, 2017. https://www.wellsfargofunds.com/assets/edocs/marketing/sales-material/uniting-happiness-and-money.pdf.

Winograd, Morley, and Michael D. Hais. "Millennial Momentum: How a New Generation is Remaking America." New Brunswick, NJ: Rutgers University Press, 2011.

Ziglar, Zig. *Great Quotes from Zig Ziglar*. New York: Gramercy. 2005.

Made in the USA
Middletown, DE
11 April 2022

64060232R00080